# also by the editors at america's test kitchen

for a full listing of all our books

CooksIllustrated.com

AmericasTestKitchen.com

# COOK'S ILLUSTRATED | all time best

# brunch

COOK'S ILLUSTRATED | all time best

# brunch

the editors at
**america's test kitchen**

Library of Congress Cataloging-in-Publication Data
Names: America's Test Kitchen (Firm), publisher.
Title: Cook's illustrated all time best brunch / the editors at America's Test Kitchen.
Other titles: All time best brunch
Description: Boston, MA : America's Test Kitchen, [2018] | Includes index.
Identifiers: LCCN 2018008949 | ISBN 9781945256608
Subjects: LCSH: Brunches. | Cooking, American.
Classification: LCC TX733 .C68334 2018 | DDC 641.5/2--dc23
LC record available at https://lccn.loc.gov/2018008949

AMERICA'S TEST KITCHEN
21 Drydock Avenue, Boston, MA 02210
Manufactured in the United States of America
10 9 8 7 6 5 4 3 2 1

Distributed by Penguin Random House Publisher Services
Tel: 800.733.3000

**Editorial Director, Books:** Elizabeth Carduff
**Executive Editor:** Adam Kowit
**Assistant Editor:** Samantha Ronan
**Editorial Assistant:** Alyssa Langer
**Design Director, Books:** Carole Goodman
**Deputy Art Director:** Jen Kanavos Hoffman
**Photography Director:** Julie Bozzo Cote
**Photography Producer:** Meredith Mulcahy
**Senior Staff Photographer:** Daniel J. van Ackere
**Staff Photographers:** Steve Klise and Kevin White
**Feature Photography:** Keller + Keller and Carl Tremblay
**Food Styling:** Catrine Kelty, Chantal Lambeth, Kendra McKnight, Marie Piraino, Elle Simone Scott, and Sally Staub
**Photoshoot Kitchen Team:**
    **Manager:** Timothy McQuinn
    **Lead Test Cook:** Daniel Cellucci
    **Test Cook:** Jessica Rudoph
    **Assistant Test Cooks:** Sarah Ewald, Eric Haessler, and Mady Nichas
**Production Director:** Guy Rochford
**Senior Production Manager:** Jessica Lindheimer Quirk
**Production Manager:** Christine Spanger
**Imaging Manager:** Lauren Robbins
**Production and Imaging Specialists:** Heather Dube, Dennis Noble, and Jessica Voas
**Copy Editor:** Cheryl Redmond
**Proofreader:** Pat Jalbert-Levine
**Indexer:** Elizabeth Parson

**Chief Creative Office:** Jack Bishop
**Executive Editorial Directors:** Julia Collin Davison and Bridget Lancaster

*Pictured on front cover:* Spinach and Feta Quiche (page 84), Peach, Blackberry, and Strawberry Fruit Salad with Basil and Pepper (page 149), Ultimate Cinnamon Buns (page 122), Oven-Fried Bacon (page 164), and Yeasted Waffles (page 45).

*Pictured on back cover:* Huevos Rancheros (page 31), Blueberry Swirl Muffins (page 103), Spicy Shrimp Skewers with Cheesy Grits (page 65), and Tricolor Salad with Balsamic Vinaigrette (page 169).

# contents

# welcome to america's test kitchen

THIS BOOK HAS BEEN TESTED, WRITTEN, AND EDITED BY THE FOLKS at America's Test Kitchen. Located in Boston's Seaport District in the historic Innovation and Design Building, it features 15,000 square feet of kitchen space including photography and video studios. It is the home of *Cook's Illustrated* magazine and *Cook's Country* magazine and is the workday destination for more than 60 test cooks, editors, and cookware specialists. Our mission is to test recipes over and over again until we understand how and why they work and until we arrive at the best version.

We start the process of testing a recipe with a complete lack of preconceptions, which means that we accept no claim, no technique, and no recipe at face value. We simply assemble as many variations as possible, test a half-dozen of the most promising, and taste the results blind. We then construct our own recipe and continue to test it, varying ingredients, techniques, and cooking times until we reach a consensus. As we like to say in the test kitchen, "We make the mistakes so you don't have to." The result, we hope, is the best version of a particular recipe, but we realize that only you can be the final judge of our success (or failure). We use the same rigorous approach when we test equipment and taste ingredients.

All of this would not be possible without a belief that good cooking, much like good music, is based on a foundation of objective technique. Some people like spicy foods and others don't, but there is a right way to sauté, there is a best way to cook a pot roast, and there are measurable scientific principles involved in producing perfectly beaten, stable egg whites. Our ultimate goal is to investigate the fundamental principles of cooking to give you the techniques, tools, and ingredients you need to become a better cook. It is as simple as that.

To see what goes on behind the scenes at America's Test Kitchen, check out our social media channels for kitchen snapshots, exclusive content, video tips, and much more. You can watch us work (in our actual test kitchen) by tuning in to *America's Test Kitchen* or *Cook's Country from America's Test Kitchen* on public television or on our websites. Listen to test kitchen experts on public radio (SplendidTable.org) to hear insights that illuminate the truth about real home cooking. Want to hone your cooking skills or finally learn how to bake—with an America's Test Kitchen test cook? Enroll in one of our online cooking classes. However you choose to visit us, we welcome you into our kitchen, where you can stand by our side as we test our way to the best recipes in America.

# introduction

EVERYBODY LOVES BRUNCH. WHETHER YOU HAVE AN INSATIABLE sweet tooth or wake up hungry for a meaty, satisfying hash or crave eggs in any and all forms, there's no denying the appeal of that leisurely, indulgent weekend meal, the perfect time to take things slow and just enjoy. For the host, however, orchestrating the perfect brunch can be a daunting juggling act. Brunch staples like eggs Benedict, pancakes, and French toast are usually time-sensitive dishes best served as soon as they're ready, while classic baked goods like coffee cake and cinnamon rolls require a lot of advance work and tedious waiting. From overcooked eggs to underproofed pastry, the challenges of pulling off a memorable brunch can quickly add a lot of stress to what should be a relaxing, laid-back affair.

Here in the test kitchen, we are firm believers in homemade brunch, and we know it doesn't have to be a maddening odyssey to get there. That's why we created this collection. Through these 75 expertly tested recipes, we make the case that brunch is better at home, and that hosting this meal is a rewarding, doable endeavor. Skeptical? Consider our French Toast Casserole (page 96). This simple recipe was tailor-made for a lazy Sunday, delivering everything we love about traditional French toast—rich custard, crisp-creamy bread, and the sweet, spiced notes of cinnamon, nutmeg, and vanilla— in a cozy, crowd-pleasing casserole that can be assembled a day in advance. Or if you're an egg lover, give our innovative Huevos Rancheros (page 31) a try. Our version streamlines brunch by building a simple sauce on a sheet pan and then clearing out wells in which we cook the eggs. Saucy, spicy, and rich, this one-pan meal is deeply satisfying; plus, it leaves your stovetop free for preparing quick sides like our crisp Hash Browns (page 157) or searing our perfectly seasoned Homemade Breakfast Sausage (page 167), an effortless recipe that can be frozen up to a month ahead of time. And those wobbly eggs Benedict you thought you could enjoy only at a restaurant? We make them entirely accessible with a stable, failproof hollandaise and easy-to-poach eggs, both of which can be refrigerated for up to three days before serving (page 10). Pair them with a crisp, fresh side like our Tricolor Salad with Balsamic Vinaigrette (page 169) or Roasted Asparagus with Mint-Orange Gremolata (page 158) and you've got a bistro-caliber brunch. And with recipes like our simple but stately Leek and Goat Cheese Quiche (page 84), our superstreamlined Croque Monsieurs (page 63), and our one-skillet Corned Beef Hash with Poached Eggs (page 67) on hand, you can confidently offer your guests fresh, flavorful homemade upgrades to all the brunch basics.

Across these chapters, we share the best of *Cook's Illustrated*'s brunch know-how through recipes that work for any and every occasion. With extensive make-ahead instructions, simple recipes for everything from cold brew coffee to bubbly cocktails, and a range of syrups and toppings to finish off even the simplest spread with finesse, this book has everything you need to make your home kitchen the newest brunch hot spot.

come
over for
brunch

# the brunch road map

## make it ahead

Hosting brunch doesn't have to mean waking at the crack of dawn to start cooking. Many of the recipes in this book allow you to prepare part of the dish ahead of time. Here are some of our favorite make-ahead tips:

**1. keep it warm** Made-to-order no more! Pancakes and waffles can be kept warm on a wire rack in a low oven and poached eggs can sit in a pot of 150-degree water until you're ready to serve.

**2. wrap in plastic or foil** Many cakes and breads will still taste fresh a few days later when properly wrapped and stored at room temperature.

**3. halfway there** From undressed salads to unrisen rolls to assembled unbaked casseroles, many recipes can be partially prepared and finished off within hours of serving.

**4. freeze it** The freezer is the brunch host's best friend. Recipes like Homemade Breakfast Sausage (page 167), Quick Coffee Cake (page 138), and Spanakopita (page 89) can be frozen and finished off weeks later.

## pack something impressive

Potlucks take the pressure off the host and allow each guest to bring something really spectacular to brunch. If you want to bring a casserole and serve it right away, bring it in an insulated food carrier for safe, stay-hot transport. The **Rachael Ray Expandable Lasagna Lugger** ($26.95) is our favorite.

Brunches come in all shapes and sizes, from casual to refined, intimate to sprawling. We've broken down this meal into a few basic lanes you can follow, but in the end, there's no wrong way to brunch.

## step one: start out strong

Give yourself time to finish up in the kitchen by putting a few things out for guests to sip and snack on until brunch is ready. Offer coffee, tea, juice, and cocktails (see pages 6–7) and have cream and sugar at the ready. Almond-Raisin Granola (page 150), set out with yogurt and bowls, and tempting bites like Ultimate Banana Bread (page 127) and Muffin Tin Doughnuts (page 116) will keep guests happy until mealtime.

## step two: plot your course to a perfect brunch

**sweet and savory kept simple** Sweet and savory is an unbeatable pairing (and one that should apply to all brunches). For a classic brunch, partner a stellar egg dish like the Family-Sized Cheese Omelet (page 19), Egg Roulade with Spinach and Gruyère (page 21), or Baked Eggs Florentine (page 12) with something sweet, like Apple Fritters (page 118) or Classic Buttermilk Pancakes (page 35). Round out the meal with a few easy sides like Oven-Fried Bacon (page 164), Tricolor Salad with Balsamic Vinaigrette (page 169), and Home Fries (page 155).

**start with a centerpiece** No matter the tenor of your brunch, sometimes it's best to start with a single showpiece at the center. Your starring dish could be something ambitious—our French Onion and Bacon Tart (page 86), for instance—or something simple but unexpected, like Ham and Cheese Waffles (page 46), a platter of Croque Monsieurs (page 63), or an eye-catching basket of baked goods. Surround your showstopper with a few understated accompaniments like Roasted Green Beans with Almonds and Mint (page 161), Baked Cheese Grits (page 152), or Peach, Blackberry, and Strawberry Fruit Salad with Basil and Pepper (page 149).

**brunching on a grand scale** Scaling brunch up to serve a crowd makes this laid-back meal a little more stressful to orchestrate, but you don't necessarily need to plan on each person taking a heaping portion of each offering. All you really need to do is pick a few hearty mains and pair them with enough sides to satisfy a crowd. Here are a few sample menus that serve 10 to 12 people—whether plated or in a buffet setting—to give you a leg up:

### an elegant holiday affair
- oven-poached salmon with lemon-dill sauce (page 72)
- tricolor salad with balsamic vinaigrette (page 169)
- roasted green beans with pecorino and pine nuts (page 161)
- crêpes with sugar and lemon (two batches, page 51)
- olive oil cake (page 143)

### a stick-to-your-ribs spread
- family-sized cheese omelet (page 19; make two if needed)
- homemade breakfast sausage (page 167)
- baked cheese grits (page 152)
- peach, blackberry, and strawberry fruit salad with basil and pepper (page 149; double recipe if needed)
- blueberry swirl muffins (page 103)

### a fancy feast
- muffin tin frittatas (page 24)
- french onion and bacon tart (page 86)
- salade niçoise (page 78)
- british-style currant scones (page 109)
- ginger-peach bellinis (page 7)

### a lazy sunday buffet
- 24-hour "omelet" (page 93)
- oven-fried bacon (page 164)
- honey-pecan granola (page 150) with yogurt and fresh fruit
- quick coffee cake (page 138)

### step three: incorporate fresh finishing touches
Before your brunch becomes too heavy, be sure to round out the meal with something fresh, crunchy, and light, like Roasted Asparagus (page 158) or Nectarine, Grape, and Blueberry Fruit Salad with Orange and Cardamom (page 149). If pancakes or waffles are on the menu, offer a few flavorful toppings and syrups for an especially sweet presentation (pages 38–39) and have some inexpensive food containers (we like **Gladware Deep Dish**, $5.97) on hand so guests can take leftovers home.

Every great brunch starts with a bracing mug of coffee or a steamy cup of tea. Any caffeine junkie knows that there's a big difference between a good and bad cup, so we have these tips and discoveries to share.

## but first, coffee

Brewing your usual morning cup may not require much thought, but when you're hosting, it's worth getting it right. Here are some key tips:

**DO buy loose beans** Buy beans in small quantities no more than a few days from their roasting date. You're more likely to get recently roasted beans from a local roaster or a store that sells them in high volume.

**DON'T buy preground coffee** Freshly ground beans make the best coffee, period. Buy beans in a heat-sealed, aluminized Mylar bag with a one-way degassing valve. Unopened, these bags keep beans fresh for up to 90 days.

**DO measure carefully** Whether you're using a French press or an automatic drip coffee machine, we recommend using 9 to 11 grams (about 2 tablespoons) of medium-grind coffee per 6 ounces of 195- to 205-degree water.

**DON'T store coffee in the refrigerator** If you plan to keep beans longer than 10 days, store them in the freezer to limit contact with air and moisture. Refrigerated coffee will pick up off-flavors.

## brewed to perfection

There's no disputing the convenience of automatic drip coffee, especially when hosting guests, but most models brew a crummy coffee. We think French press coffee is worth the effort for a standout cup with brunch.

### cold-brew coffee concentrate
*makes about 1½ cups; enough for 3 cups iced coffee*

**9 ounces medium-roast coffee beans, ground coarse (3½ cups)**

**3½ cups filtered water, room temperature**

**Kosher salt (optional)**

**1.** Stir coffee and water together in large (about 2-quart) French press. Allow raft of ground coffee to form, about 10 minutes, then stir again to recombine. Cover with plastic wrap and let sit at room temperature for 24 hours.

**2.** Line fine-mesh strainer with coffee filter and set over large liquid measuring cup. Place lid on press and slowly and evenly press plunger down on grounds to separate them from coffee concentrate. Pour concentrate into prepared strainer. Line large bowl with triple layer of cheesecloth, with cheesecloth overhanging edges of bowl. Transfer grounds to cheesecloth. Gather edges of cheesecloth together and twist; then, holding pouch over strainer, firmly squeeze grounds until liquid no longer runs freely from pouch; discard grounds.

**3.** Using back of ladle or rubber spatula, gently stir concentrate to help filter it through strainer. (Concentrate can be refrigerated for up to 1 week.)

### to make iced coffee
Combine equal parts coffee concentrate and cold water. Add pinch kosher salt, if using, and pour into glass with ice.

**french press**
Because the oils are not filtered out, French presses yield coffee nearly as full-bodied as espresso. The **Bodum Columbia French Press Coffee Maker, Double Wall, 8 Cup** ($79.95) is ideal for brunch because it keeps the coffee hotter longer—perfect for serving coffee as guests arrive.

**automatic drip**
The **Technivorm Moccamaster 10-Cup Coffee Maker with Thermal Carafe** ($299) and the **Bonavita 8-Cup Coffee Maker with Thermal Carafe** ($189.99) brew perfectly full-flavored coffee because they successfully send 195- to 205-degree water over the grounds in 2 to 8 minutes.

## perfecting tea time

A good tea infuser or kettle can make a big difference in the quality of your tea, but there are a number of other steps that you can take to ensure that you always brew a proper cuppa.

**it starts with water** Good water makes good tea. If your tap water is hard, run it through a filter, or use bottled water instead.

**take the temperature** White and green teas should be made with water that is well under boiling—160 to 180 degrees—and black and herbal teas are best made with water that's just under a boil, about 210 degrees.

**steep and sip** The amount of tea and the time you steep it depend in part on personal preference. Loose-leaf teas can vary in density, so weigh out the amount you need—we recommend starting with 2 to 3 grams of tea per 8 ounces of water. The smaller the leaf, the less you'll need and the faster it will infuse the water, so adjust your portion and timing accordingly. Start by steeping for 1 minute, tasting it, and then letting it steep longer, tasting as you go, until it meets your approval.

## tools of the tea trade

### tea infuser

The **Finum Brewing Basket L** ($9.95) is our favorite infuser. This basket-style strainer's tightly woven mesh keeps even the finest leaves out of the tea and its generous size easily holds up to 13.5 tablespoons of leaves. It also boasts a wide 2.5-inch opening, making it easy to fill and clean.

### stovetop kettle

Lightweight and easy to fill, the **OXO Good Grips Classic Tea Kettle in Brushed Stainless Steel** ($39.95) is a sturdy 1.7-quart kettle with a grippy, comfortable handle, a gently curved spout for smooth pouring, and an assertive whistle that can be turned off if desired.

### best iced tea

*serves 4 to 6*
*Doubling this recipe is easy, but use a large saucepan and expect the water to take longer to reach the proper temperature. For a stronger iced tea, reduce the amount of ice to 3 cups. Garnish with lemon wedges if desired.*

**5 black tea bags**

**4 cups water**

**1–6 tablespoons sugar**

**4 cups ice cubes, plus more for serving**

Tie strings of tea bags together and heat with water in medium sauce-pan over medium heat until dark colored, very steamy, and small bubbles form on bottom and sides of pan (tea will register about 190 degrees), 10 to 15 minutes. Off heat, let steep for 3 minutes (no longer or tea may become bitter). Remove tea bags; pour tea into pitcher. Stir in sugar to taste, then stir in ice until melted. Serve in ice-filled glasses.

### variations
#### minted iced tea
Add ¼ cup fresh mint leaves, bruised with wooden spoon, to saucepan along with tea bags and water. When steeping is complete, remove tea bags and strain tea through fine-mesh strainer to remove mint.

#### gingered iced tea
Add one 1-inch piece fresh ginger, sliced thin and smashed with broad side of large chef's knife, to saucepan along with tea bags and water. When steeping is complete, remove tea bags and strain through fine-mesh strainer to remove ginger.

# brunch-ready beverages

Coffee is only the start. From bubbly mimosas to creamy hot chocolate, no brunch is complete without a few indulgent drinks on the table.

## bloody marys

*serves 12*

*We prefer to use Campbell's Tomato Juice here, but V8 or Clamato juice can be used. To make lemon twists, take a ½-inch wide, 1½-inch long, shallow swipe of lemon zest with a vegetable peeler, avoiding the bitter white pith. Use refrigerated prepared horseradish, not the shelf-stable kind or horseradish cream. Boar's Head Pure Horseradish is our favorite prepared horseradish.*

9 cups tomato juice

3 cups vodka

¾ cup lemon juice, plus lemon wedges or twists for serving (5 lemons)

3 tablespoons Worcestershire sauce

2 tablespoons prepared horseradish

1 tablespoon salt

1 tablespoon pepper

¾ teaspoon hot sauce

Ice cubes

12 celery ribs, trimmed

Whisk tomato juice, vodka, lemon juice, Worcestershire, horseradish, salt, pepper, and hot sauce together in 4-quart pitcher or large bowl. Pour over ice and garnish with celery and lemon wedges or twists before serving.

**to make ahead**
Bloody Marys can be refrigerated for up to 8 hours.

## mimosas

*serves 6 to 8*

*To make orange twists, take a ½-inch wide, 1½-inch long, shallow swipe of orange zest with a vegetable peeler, avoiding the bitter white pith.*

**1 (750-ml) bottle prosecco or champagne**

**3 cups orange juice**

**Orange slices or twists**

Combine all ingredients in large pitcher and serve chilled. Garnish with orange slices or twists.

### variation

rose blossom mimosas

Omit orange slices. Add ½ teaspoon rose blossom water. Garnish with rose petals.

## bellinis

*serves 6 to 8*

**1 (750-ml) bottle prosecco or champagne**

**1½ cups peach juice**

**Peach slices**

Combine all ingredients in large pitcher and serve chilled. Garnish with peach slices.

### variation

ginger-peach bellinis

Combine peach nectar and 1½ teaspoons grated fresh ginger in bowl, then immediately strain through fine-mesh strainer into large pitcher. Add prosecco and serve chilled.

## decadent hot chocolate

*serves 4*

*You can substitute 4 ounces of your favorite semisweet or bittersweet chocolate bar for the chocolate chips. For an adult treat, add a bit of Tía Maria, peppermint schnapps, Kahlúa, or Grand Marnier before serving. This recipe can be doubled.*

**3 cups milk**

**1 cup heavy cream**

**2 tablespoons Dutch-processed cocoa powder**

**1 tablespoon sugar**

**½ cup semisweet chocolate chips**

**1 teaspoon vanilla extract**

Bring milk, cream, cocoa powder, and sugar to boil in medium saucepan. Off heat, stir in chocolate and vanilla. Cover, let chips melt for about 1 minute, then whisk smooth before serving.

**to make ahead**

Cooled hot chocolate can be refrigerated, covered tightly with plastic wrap, for up to 24 hours before serving. Reheat in microwave or in medium saucepan set over low heat.

## chai

*serves 4*

*Depending on how sweet you like your chai, you will need to add between 1 and 2 tablespoons of sugar to the milk mixture in step 1. Any type of supermarket black tea will work here. For an accurate measurement of boiling water, bring a full kettle of water to a boil and then measure out the desired amount.*

**1⅓ cups milk**

**1 cinnamon stick, broken in half**

**½ teaspoon vanilla extract**

**¼ teaspoon ground cardamom**

**¼ teaspoon whole black peppercorns**

**¼ teaspoon whole cloves**

**2 tablespoons sugar**

**3 cups boiling water**

**4 black tea bags**

**1.** Simmer milk, cinnamon, vanilla, cardamom, peppercorns, and cloves in medium saucepan over medium-low heat for 5 minutes. Off heat, stir in 1 tablespoon sugar until dissolved, add remaining sugar to taste, and strain spiced milk through fine-mesh strainer. Discard peppercorns and cloves.

**2.** Meanwhile, divide boiling water among 4 mugs and place 1 tea bag in each. Let steep for about 5 minutes. Remove tea bags and pour ⅓ cup spiced warm milk into each mug.

# eggs
# every
# way

# eggs benedict

*why this recipe works* Eggs Benedict is a treat usually reserved for restaurant dining, but this recipe makes it doable at home. We prepared an extra-stable hollandaise by whisking butter, yolks, and water in a double boiler, adding lemon juice off the heat. We kept the poached eggs neat by draining their loose whites in a colander and bolstering the water with vinegar to set the whites. An instant-read thermometer is essential for making the sauce. For an accurate measurement of boiling water, bring a full kettle of water to a boil and then measure out the desired amount.

*serves 4*
*total time: 45 minutes*

**8 tablespoons unsalted butter, cut into 8 pieces and softened**

**8 large eggs and 4 large egg yolks**

**⅓ cup boiling water**

**2 teaspoons lemon juice**

**Salt**

**Pinch cayenne pepper**

**1 tablespoon distilled white vinegar**

**4 English muffins, split**

**8 slices Canadian bacon**

1. Place butter and egg yolks in large heat-resistant glass or ceramic bowl. Bring ½ inch water to simmer in medium saucepan. Place bowl over simmering water, making sure that water does not touch bottom of bowl, and whisk constantly until mixture is smooth and homogeneous, about 1 minute.

2. Slowly add boiling water and cook, whisking constantly, until thickened and sauce registers 160 degrees, 7 to 10 minutes.

3. Off heat, whisk in lemon juice, ⅛ teaspoon salt, and cayenne. Remove saucepan from heat (keep bowl over water bath) and season with salt to taste. Cover to keep warm.

4. Adjust oven rack 6 inches from broiler element and heat broiler. Bring 6 cups water to boil in Dutch oven over high heat. Fill large pot with water and heat over high heat until water reaches 150 degrees, about 10 minutes (water will be steaming, and small bubbles will be visible). Remove from heat and cover to keep warm.

5. Meanwhile, crack 4 eggs into colander, taking care not to break yolks. Let stand until loose, watery whites drain away from eggs, 20 to 30 seconds. Gently transfer eggs to 2-cup liquid measuring cup.

6. Add vinegar and 1 teaspoon salt to boiling water. With lip of measuring cup just above surface of water, gently tip eggs into water, one at a time, leaving space between them. Cover Dutch oven, remove from heat, and let stand until whites closest to yolks are just set and opaque, about 3 minutes. If after 3 minutes whites are not set, let stand in water, checking every 30 seconds, until eggs reach desired doneness. (For medium-cooked yolks, leave covered for 4 minutes, then begin checking for doneness.) Using slotted spoon, carefully transfer each egg to pot with 150-degree water; cover and keep warm.

7. Return water in Dutch oven to boil. Repeat draining and cooking remaining 4 eggs and transfer to pot with 150-degree water; cover and keep warm.

8. Arrange English muffins split side up on baking sheet and broil until golden brown, 2 to 4 minutes. Place 1 slice bacon on each muffin half and broil until hot and beginning to brown, about 1 minute. Remove sheet from oven.

9. Working with one at a time, carefully lift and drain each egg and arrange on top of each muffin half. Spoon 1 to 2 tablespoons sauce over each egg. Serve, passing remaining sauce separately.

**to make ahead**
Sauce can be held at room temperature for up to 1 hour or refrigerated for up to 3 days; before serving, microwave on 50 percent power for 1 minute, stirring every 10 seconds, until heated through. Poached eggs can be refrigerated in bowl of cold water for up to 3 days. To reheat, heat 6 cups water to 150 degrees, transfer eggs to water, and cover for 3 minutes.

# baked eggs florentine

*why this recipe works* Baked eggs are a humble but rich brunch main, and our version brings an air of elegance to the table while also keeping things convenient. Rather than fuss with a water bath or finicky baking times, we kept things hands-off, relying instead on nests of rich spinach cream sauce to insulate the eggs from overcooking, harnessing the residual heat trapped in the walls of the ramekins to gently bring them to ideal doneness. We boosted a quick cream sauce with spinach, Parmesan, and spices and baked it in individual ramekins to get it good and hot. We then pressed a divot into each mound of sauce, slid an egg into each, and baked the eggs until they were nearly done, letting carryover cooking finish them off as they rested. Be sure to add the eggs to the hot filling–lined ramekins quickly. Use 6-ounce ramekins with 3¼-inch diameters, measured from the inner lip. Remove the eggs from the oven when the whites have just turned opaque but are still jiggly. We developed this recipe using a glass baking dish; if using a metal baking pan, reduce the oven temperature to 425 degrees. This recipe can be doubled: Bake the ramekins in two 13 by 9-inch dishes and increase the baking times in steps 2 and 3 by 1 minute.

*serves 6*
*total time: 1 hour*

**2 tablespoons unsalted butter**

**1 large shallot, minced**

**1 tablespoon all-purpose flour**

**¾ cup half-and-half**

**10 ounces frozen spinach, thawed and squeezed dry**

**2 ounces Parmesan cheese, grated (1 cup)**

**Salt and pepper**

**⅛ teaspoon dry mustard**

**⅛ teaspoon ground nutmeg**

**Pinch cayenne pepper**

**Vegetable oil spray**

**6 large eggs**

**1.** Adjust oven rack to middle position and heat oven to 500 degrees. Melt butter in medium saucepan over medium heat. Add shallot and cook, stirring occasionally, until softened, about 3 minutes. Stir in flour and cook, stirring constantly, for 1 minute. Gradually whisk in half-and-half; bring mixture to boil, whisking constantly. Simmer, whisking frequently, until thickened, 2 to 3 minutes. Off heat, stir in spinach, Parmesan, ¾ teaspoon salt, ½ teaspoon pepper, mustard, nutmeg, and cayenne.

**2.** Lightly spray six 6-ounce ramekins with oil spray. Evenly divide spinach filling among ramekins. Using back of spoon, push filling 1 inch up sides of ramekins to create ⅛-inch-thick layer. Shape remaining filling in bottom of ramekin into 1½ inch–diameter mound, making shallow indentation in center of mound large enough to hold yolk. Place filled ramekins in 13 by 9-inch glass baking dish. Bake until filling just starts to brown, about 7 minutes, rotating dish halfway through baking.

**3.** While filling is heating, crack eggs (taking care not to break yolks) into individual cups or bowls. Remove dish with ramekins from oven and place on wire rack. Gently pour eggs from cups into hot ramekins, centering yolk in filling. Lightly spray surface of each egg with oil spray and sprinkle each evenly with pinch salt. Return dish to oven and bake until whites are just opaque but still tremble (carry-over heat will cook whites through), 6 to 8 minutes, rotating dish halfway through baking.

**4.** Remove dish from oven and, using tongs, transfer ramekins to wire rack. Let stand until whites are firm and set (yolks should still be runny), about 10 minutes. Serve immediately.

**to make ahead**
Follow recipe through step 2, skipping baking of lined ramekins. Wrap ramekins with plastic wrap and refrigerate for up to 3 days. To serve, remove plastic and heat lined ramekins, directly from refrigerator, for additional 3 to 4 minutes (10 to 11 minutes total) before proceeding with recipe.

# scrambled eggs with goat cheese, arugula, and sun-dried tomatoes

*why this recipe works* The secret to our hearty veggie scramble—which features light, fluffy eggs dotted with oozy bites of goat cheese and plenty of tender vegetables—is keeping excess moisture at bay. We managed to incorporate add-ins without hurting the eggs' texture by carefully selecting ingredients that would minimize wetness. Leafy arugula, sun-dried tomatoes (patted dry), and tangy crumbled goat cheese all fit the bill while instantly boosting the scramble's flavor profile. After wilting the arugula in the skillet with chopped onion and red pepper flakes, we wiped the pan clean and began to cook our eggs. Whisking eggs with milk is an easy way to keep scrambled eggs tender, but here we opted for half-and-half for a richer taste with a little less moisture. We cooked the mixture gently—pushing and stirring the eggs to allow large curds to form—then simply folded in the mix-ins off heat and sprinkled on the goat cheese to finish.

*serves 4 to 6*
*total time: 20 minutes*

12 large eggs

6 tablespoons half-and-half

Salt and pepper

2 teaspoons extra-virgin olive oil

½ onion, chopped fine

⅛ teaspoon red pepper flakes

5 ounces (5 cups) baby arugula

1 tablespoon unsalted butter

¼ cup oil-packed sun-dried tomatoes, rinsed, patted dry, and chopped fine

3 ounces goat cheese, crumbled (¾ cup)

1. Beat eggs, half-and-half, ¾ teaspoon salt, and ¼ teaspoon pepper with fork in bowl until thoroughly combined.

2. Heat oil in 12-inch nonstick skillet over medium heat until shimmering. Add onion and pepper flakes and cook until onion has softened, about 5 minutes. Add arugula and cook, stirring gently, until arugula begins to wilt, 30 to 60 seconds. Spread mixture in single layer on plate.

3. Wipe out now-empty skillet with paper towels, add butter, and melt over medium heat, swirling to coat pan. Add egg mixture. Using heat-resistant rubber spatula, stir eggs constantly, slowly pushing them from side to side, scraping along bottom and sides of skillet, and lifting and folding eggs as they form curds (do not overscramble or curds formed will be too small). Cook until large curds form but eggs are still very moist, 2 to 3 minutes.

4. Off heat, gently fold in arugula mixture and sun-dried tomatoes until evenly distributed; if eggs are still underdone, return skillet to medium heat for no longer than 30 seconds. Season with salt and pepper to taste. Divide eggs among individual plates and sprinkle with goat cheese. Serve.

### variation

**scrambled eggs with zucchini, feta, and mint**
Omit red pepper flakes, arugula, and sun-dried tomatoes. Add 1 large zucchini, cut into ¼-inch pieces, to skillet with onion in step 2, and cook until crisp-tender, about 4 minutes. In step 4, off heat, fold zucchini mixture and 1½ tablespoons minced fresh mint into eggs until evenly distributed. Substitute crumbled feta cheese for goat cheese.

# migas

*why this recipe works* Migas is classic Tex-Mex fare, combining tender scrambled eggs with flavorful bites of peppers and onion, and the crisp-chewy crunch of fried tortillas for a supremely satisfying scramble. Shallow frying the tortillas (rather than simply opening a bag of chips, as some recipes do) proved essential to adding texture and deep corn flavor to the dish. As soon as the tortilla strips turned an appealing golden brown, we added onion, red bell pepper, and briny pickled jalapeños to the skillet, softening them in the oil before adding the eggs. The toasty oil along with the tortilla strips' rich corn notes infused the eggs with flavor for an authentic Tex-Mex backbone. To deliver eggs with a soft, fluffy texture, we employed a two-step cooking technique: Starting out over medium-high heat created steam to puff up the curds, and finishing them over low ensured that the eggs didn't overcook. Shredded Monterey Jack cheese, folded in at the end, offered a creamy, cohesive finish. It's important to follow the visual cues when making the eggs, as your pan's thickness will affect the cooking time. If you're using an electric stove, heat a second burner on low and move the skillet to it when it's time to adjust the heat. For a spicier dish, use the larger amount of jarred jalapeños.

*serves 4*
*total time: 30 minutes*

8 large eggs

½ teaspoon salt

¼ teaspoon pepper

3 tablespoons vegetable oil

6 (6-inch) corn tortillas, cut into 1 by ½-inch strips

1 onion, chopped fine

1 small red bell pepper, stemmed, seeded, and chopped fine

1–2 tablespoons minced jarred jalapeños

1½ ounces Monterey Jack cheese, shredded (⅓ cup), plus extra for serving

1 tablespoon chopped fresh cilantro

Salsa

1. Beat eggs, ¼ teaspoon salt, and ¼ teaspoon pepper with fork in bowl until thoroughly combined, about 1 minute; set aside.

2. Heat oil in 12-inch nonstick skillet over medium-high heat until shimmering. Add tortillas and ¼ teaspoon salt and cook, stirring occasionally, until golden brown, 4 to 6 minutes. Add onion, bell pepper, and jalapeños and cook, stirring occasionally, until vegetables are softened, 5 to 7 minutes.

3. Add egg mixture and, using heat-resistant rubber spatula, constantly and firmly scrape along bottom and sides of skillet until eggs begin to clump and spatula leaves trail on bottom of skillet, 30 to 60 seconds.

4. Reduce heat to low and gently but constantly fold egg mixture until clumped and still slightly wet, 30 to 60 seconds. Off heat, gently fold in Monterey Jack and cilantro. Serve immediately, passing salsa and extra Monterey Jack separately.

# family-sized cheese omelet

*why this recipe works* Cheese omelets are a brunch staple, but cooking up individual omelets is a chore when preparing a big spread. This oversized version—with its tender eggs and gooey cheddar filling—satisfies the whole family in one go. Flipping a huge eight-egg omelet was cumbersome work, so we developed an easy method for cooking both the top and bottom without any tricky maneuvers. After gently cooking the eggs in a warm skillet, stirring and pulling them until the bottom was just set, we covered the pan. The trapped heat and moisture steamed the top of the omelet, keeping it moist as it cooked through. We took the omelet off the heat, sprinkled shredded cheddar cheese over the surface, and covered it again, allowing the cheese to melt before we slid and folded our omelet onto a platter. Sliced into generous, cheesy wedges, this one-for-all omelet was sheer perfection. Monterey Jack, Colby, or any other good melting cheese can be substituted for the cheddar. Finish with minced fresh herbs if desired. You will need a 12-inch nonstick skillet with a tight-fitting lid for this recipe.

*serves 4*
*total time: 20 minutes*

8 large eggs

½ teaspoon salt

¼ teaspoon pepper

2 tablespoons unsalted butter

3 ounces sharp cheddar cheese, shredded (¾ cup)

1. Whisk eggs, salt, and pepper together in bowl. Melt butter in 12-inch nonstick skillet over medium heat, swirling to coat pan. Add eggs and cook, stirring gently in circular motion, until mixture is slightly thickened, about 1 minute.

2. Using heat-resistant rubber spatula, gently pull cooked eggs back from edge of skillet and tilt pan, allowing any uncooked egg to run to cleared edge of skillet. Repeat this process, working your way around skillet, until bottom of omelet is just set but top is still runny, about 1 minute. Cover skillet, reduce heat to low, and cook until top of omelet begins to set but is still moist, about 5 minutes.

3. Off heat, sprinkle with cheddar, cover, and let sit until cheese partially melts, about 1 minute. Using rubber spatula, slide half of omelet onto serving platter, then tilt skillet so remaining omelet flips over onto itself. Cut into wedges and serve immediately.

## variations

### family-sized omelet with tomato, bacon, and garlic
Omit butter. Before cooking eggs, cook 8 slices finely chopped bacon in 12-inch nonstick skillet over medium-high heat until brown and crisp, 5 to 7 minutes; transfer to paper towel–lined plate. Pour off all but 2 tablespoons fat left in pan, add 1 finely chopped tomato and ½ finely chopped green bell pepper and cook over medium-high heat until softened, about 6 minutes. Stir in 4 minced garlic cloves and cook until fragrant, about 30 seconds. Reduce heat to medium, add eggs and bacon to vegetables in pan, and cook omelet as directed.

### family-sized omelet with arugula, sun-dried tomatoes, and provolone
Substitute provolone cheese for cheddar. Before cooking eggs, cook 1 finely chopped onion, 1 tablespoon olive oil, and ⅛ teaspoon red pepper flakes in 12-inch nonstick skillet over medium-high heat until onion is softened, about 5 minutes. Stir in ¼ cup oil-packed sun-dried tomatoes, patted dry and chopped fine. Add 5 cups baby arugula, a handful at a time, until wilted, about 1 minute. Reduce heat to medium, add butter and eggs to vegetables in pan, and cook omelet as directed.

# egg roulade with spinach and gruyère

*why this recipe works* Striking yet simple, this egg roulade puts an upscale spin on the everyday omelet, offering a light, fluffy texture, rich flavor, and a stunning presentation for an elegant brunch centerpiece. Traditional approaches call for the tedious task of preparing a roux and carefully whisking it into egg yolks for a delicate, foamy base, but we reached a similar end with a far simpler approach. After whisking a dozen eggs and seasoning them with minced garlic, salt, and pepper, we gently incorporated half-and-half for rich, tender eggs and flour for structure. We poured the egg mixture into a parchment-lined sheet pan and, rather than preparing a filling separately, sprinkled the surface with convenient frozen chopped spinach. After less than 10 minutes in the oven, our enriched eggs emerged airy, nicely set, and swirled with tender spinach. Nutty Gruyère pairs well with spinach and wouldn't weigh down the roulade with additional moisture, so we sprinkled it evenly over the still-warm surface before carefully rolling it into its stately signature shape. Following the instructions for lining the baking sheet with overhanging parchment paper is crucial to the success of this dish. You can substitute whole milk for the half-and-half in this recipe, but the eggs will be less rich and less tender.

*serves 4 to 6*
*total time: 30 minutes*

12 large eggs

1 garlic clove, minced to paste

¼ teaspoon salt

⅛ teaspoon pepper

¼ cup half-and-half

2 tablespoons all-purpose flour

8 ounces frozen chopped spinach, thawed and squeezed dry

4 ounces Gruyère cheese, shredded (1 cup)

**1.** Adjust oven rack to middle position and heat oven to 375 degrees. Grease rimmed baking sheet with vegetable oil spray, then press sheet of parchment paper into baking sheet, making sure to get paper into corners and up sides. Coat parchment with vegetable oil spray.

**2.** Whisk eggs, garlic, salt, and pepper together in large bowl. In separate bowl, whisk half-and-half and flour together, then slowly whisk into egg mixture until uniform. Carefully pour egg mixture into prepared baking sheet and sprinkle spinach over top. Bake until eggs are just set, about 9 minutes, rotating baking sheet halfway through baking.

**3.** Remove pan from oven and immediately sprinkle Gruyère over top. Using parchment paper and starting on one long side, lift and roll egg over itself into tight cylinder. Gently roll roulade backward into middle of parchment paper, then use parchment as sling to transfer roulade to cutting board. Slice and serve.

**variation**

egg roulade with goat cheese and sun-dried tomatoes
Sprinkle 3 tablespoons chopped oil-packed sun-dried tomatoes over eggs with spinach. Substitute 1 cup crumbled goat cheese for Gruyère.

# broccoli and feta frittata

*why this recipe works* Frittatas offer an easy route to a satisfying brunch, and ours is brimming with full-flavored vegetables and oozy bites of cheese. We ensured cohesive eggs cooked evenly from top to bottom and a distinct, hearty filling by adopting a hybrid skillet-oven cooking technique and carefully preparing the mix-ins. For a vegetable filling that was tender and remained suspended in the eggs, we chopped broccoli florets into small pieces and imparted some flavor-boosting browning on the stovetop before adding the eggs to the skillet. Red pepper flakes and lemon zest and juice offered a bright, spicy boost. Whisking milk into the eggs kept them tender, and by stirring and scraping the mixture as it cooked, we distributed the curds evenly for a perfectly tender frittata. Adding in some crumbled feta offered bites of bright, briny flavor. As soon as the skillet was filled with partially cooked curds, we smoothed out the surface and transferred the frittata to the more gentle heat of the oven to finish it off. This frittata can be served warm or at room temperature.

*serves 4 to 6*
*total time: 30 minutes*

12 large eggs

⅓ cup whole milk

Salt

1 tablespoon extra-virgin olive oil

12 ounces broccoli florets, cut into ½-inch pieces (4 cups)

Pinch red pepper flakes

3 tablespoons water

½ teaspoon grated lemon zest plus ½ teaspoon juice

4 ounces feta cheese, crumbled into ½-inch pieces (1 cup)

1. Adjust oven rack to middle position and heat oven to 350 degrees. Whisk eggs, milk, and ½ teaspoon salt in bowl until well combined.

2. Heat oil in 12-inch ovensafe nonstick skillet over medium-high heat until shimmering. Add broccoli, pepper flakes, and ¼ teaspoon salt; cook, stirring frequently, until broccoli is crisp-tender and spotty brown, 7 to 9 minutes. Add water and lemon zest and juice; continue to cook, stirring constantly, until broccoli is just tender and no water remains in skillet, about 1 minute longer.

3. Add feta and egg mixture and cook, using rubber spatula to stir and scrape bottom of skillet until large curds form and spatula leaves trail through eggs but eggs are still very wet, about 30 seconds. Smooth curds into even layer and cook, without stirring, for 30 seconds. Transfer skillet to oven and bake until frittata is slightly puffy and surface bounces back when lightly pressed, 6 to 9 minutes. Using rubber spatula, loosen frittata from skillet and transfer to cutting board. Let stand for 5 minutes before slicing and serving.

### variations

asparagus and goat cheese frittata
*This recipe works best with thin and medium-size asparagus.*

Substitute 1 pound asparagus, trimmed and cut into ¼-inch pieces, for broccoli and ¼ teaspoon pepper for pepper flakes. Reduce cooking time in step 2 to 3 to 4 minutes. Omit water. Substitute goat cheese for feta and add 2 tablespoons chopped fresh mint to eggs with cheese.

shiitake mushroom frittata with pecorino romano
*While the shiitake mushrooms needn't be cut into exact ½-inch pieces, for a cohesive frittata, make sure that no pieces are much larger than ¾ inch.*

Substitute 1 pound shiitake mushrooms, stemmed and cut into ½-inch pieces, for broccoli and ¼ teaspoon pepper for pepper flakes. Reduce water to 2 tablespoons and substitute 2 minced scallion whites, 1 tablespoon sherry vinegar, and 1½ teaspoons minced fresh thyme for lemon zest and juice. Substitute ¾ cup shredded Pecorino Romano for feta and add 2 thinly sliced scallion greens to eggs with cheese.

# muffin tin frittatas

*why this recipe works* These miniature frittatas are easy enough to make on a weekday, but their hand-held size makes them the perfect addition to a sumptuous Sunday brunch. The key to success lay in preventing the pint-size frittatas from sticking to the pan. In addition to spraying a nonstick tin with oil, we also enriched the eggs with half-and-half, the increased fat ensuring a clean release. We prepared two fillings, leaving the option to mix and match frittata flavors across a single tin. Ladling the custardy egg mixture over the filling was all the assembly needed, and these frittatas baked up beautifully in minutes. Make two different types of frittatas in a single muffin tin by making half-batches of each filling: Halve the ingredients, use a 10-inch skillet, and reduce the cooking time to 8 to 10 minutes.

*makes 12 muffins*
*total time: 30 minutes*
*(plus 10 minutes cooling time)*

8 large eggs

¼ cup half-and-half

½ teaspoon pepper

¼ teaspoon salt

1 recipe filling (recipes follow)

**1.** Adjust oven rack to lower-middle position and heat oven to 425 degrees. Generously spray 12-cup nonstick muffin tin with vegetable oil spray. Whisk eggs, half-and-half, pepper, and salt together in large bowl.

**2.** Divide filling evenly among muffin cups. Using ladle, evenly distribute egg mixture over filling in muffin cups. Bake until frittatas are lightly puffed and just set in centers, 9 to 11 minutes. Transfer muffin tin to wire rack and let frittatas cool for 10 minutes. Run plastic knife around edges of frittatas, if necessary, to loosen from muffin tin, then gently remove and serve.

chorizo, parsley, and pepper jack filling
*makes 4 cups*

1 tablespoon olive oil

8 ounces Spanish-style chorizo sausage, quartered lengthwise and sliced thin

8 ounces Yukon Gold potatoes, unpeeled, quartered lengthwise and sliced thin

1 large onion, chopped fine

½ teaspoon salt

2 garlic cloves, minced

6 ounces pepper Jack cheese, shredded (1½ cups)

3 tablespoons minced fresh parsley

Heat oil in 12-inch nonstick skillet over medium heat until shimmering. Add chorizo, potatoes, onion, and salt and cook, stirring occasionally, until potatoes are tender, 10 to 15 minutes. Stir in garlic and cook until fragrant, about 30 seconds. Transfer to bowl and let cool for 15 minutes. Stir in pepper Jack and parsley.

mushroom, chive, and gruyère filling
*makes 4 cups*

2 tablespoons olive oil

10 ounces cremini mushrooms, trimmed and sliced thin

8 ounces Yukon Gold potatoes, unpeeled, quartered lengthwise and sliced thin

1 large onion, chopped fine

½ teaspoon salt

2 garlic cloves, minced

6 ounces Gruyère cheese, shredded (1½ cups)

3 tablespoons minced fresh chives

Heat oil in 12-inch nonstick skillet over medium heat until shimmering. Add mushrooms, potatoes, onion, and salt and cook, stirring occasionally, until potatoes are tender, 10 to 15 minutes. Stir in garlic and cook until fragrant, about 30 seconds. Transfer to bowl and let cool for 15 minutes. Stir in Gruyère and chives.

**to make ahead**
Egg mixture and filling can be prepared up to 24 hours in advance; refrigerate them separately.

# spanish tortilla with chorizo and scallions

*why this recipe works* Spanish tortilla is a classic tapa, but its creamy eggs, tender potatoes, and smoky chorizo make it perfect for brunch as well. Browning the chorizo before adding the potatoes infused the spuds with smoky flavor. After combining the potatoes and eggs, we cooked the tortilla in a skillet, covering it to trap the heat before flipping it to cook the other side. Serve warm or at room temperature with Garlic Mayonnaise (recipe follows). Use a cured, Spanish-style chorizo for this recipe. Portuguese linguiça sausage is a suitable substitute.

*serves 4 to 6*
*total time: 45 minutes*
*(plus 15 minutes cooling time)*

1½ pounds Yukon Gold potatoes, peeled, quartered, and sliced ⅛ inch thick

1 small onion, halved and sliced thin

5 tablespoons plus 1 teaspoon extra-virgin olive oil

Salt and pepper

4 ounces Spanish-style chorizo, cut into ¼-inch pieces

8 large eggs

4 scallions, green and white parts sliced thin

**1.** Toss potatoes, onion, ¼ cup oil, ½ teaspoon salt, and ¼ teaspoon pepper in large bowl until potatoes are thoroughly separated and coated in oil. Heat chorizo and 1 tablespoon oil in 10-inch non-stick skillet over medium-high heat, stirring occasionally, until chorizo is browned and fat has rendered, about 5 minutes. Reduce heat to medium-low and add potato mixture to skillet. Cover potato mixture and cook, stirring with heat-resistant rubber spatula every 5 minutes, until potatoes offer no resistance when poked with paring knife, 22 to 28 minutes (some potatoes may break into smaller pieces).

**2.** Meanwhile, whisk eggs and ½ teaspoon salt in now-empty bowl until just combined. Using rubber spatula, fold hot potato mixture and scallions into eggs until combined, making sure to scrape all of potato mixture out of skillet. Return skillet to medium-high heat, add remaining 1 teaspoon oil, and heat until just beginning to smoke. Add egg-potato mixture and cook, shaking pan and folding mixture constantly for 15 seconds. Smooth top of mixture with rubber spatula. Reduce heat to medium, cover, and cook, gently shaking pan every 30 seconds, until bottom is golden brown and top is lightly set, about 2 minutes.

**3.** Using rubber spatula, loosen tortilla from pan, shaking back and forth until tortilla slides around freely in pan. Slide tortilla onto large plate, invert onto second large plate, and slide, browned side up, back into skillet. Tuck edges of tortilla into skillet with rubber spatula. Return pan to medium heat and continue to cook, gently shaking pan every 30 seconds, until second side is golden brown, about 2 minutes longer.

**4.** Slide tortilla onto cutting board or serving plate and let cool for at least 15 minutes. Cut tortilla into wedges and serve.

### garlic mayonnaise
*makes about 1¼ cups*

2 large egg yolks

2 teaspoons Dijon mustard

2 teaspoons lemon juice

1 garlic clove, minced

¾ cup vegetable oil

1 tablespoon water

½ teaspoon salt

¼ teaspoon pepper

¼ cup extra-virgin olive oil

Process egg yolks, mustard, lemon juice, and garlic in food processor until combined, about 10 seconds. With processor running, slowly drizzle in vegetable oil, about 1 minute. Transfer mixture to medium bowl and whisk in water, salt, and pepper. Whisking constantly, slowly drizzle in olive oil.

**to make ahead**
Garlic Mayonnaise can be refrigerated for up to 4 days.

# shakshuka

*why this recipe works* Aromatic, comforting, and a breeze to prepare, shakshuka is a humble Tunisian skillet meal of poached eggs quivering in a spiced tomato, onion, and pepper sauce. To bring the perfect balance of piquancy, acidity, richness, and sweetness home, we started by creating a pantry-friendly base for the sauce, sautéing onion and yellow bell pepper before incorporating a handful of fragrant, contrasting spices and umami-boosting tomato paste. Canned piquillo peppers instantly contributed some authentic wood fire–smoked flavor. To build this base into a rich sauce, we added canned diced tomatoes and their juice as well as some water, simmered the mixture to a thick consistency, and then pureed a portion of the sauce until velvety smooth. To finish, we stirred the puree back into the sauce and poached eight eggs directly in it, covering the pan to contain the heat for efficient, even cooking. A sprinkling of bright cilantro and salty, creamy feta cheese offered a fresh finish. Jarred roasted red peppers can be substituted for the piquillo peppers. Serve with pita or crusty bread to mop up the sauce. You will need a 12-inch skillet with a tight-fitting lid for this recipe.

*serves 4*
*total time: 1 hour*

3 tablespoons vegetable oil

2 onions, chopped fine

2 yellow bell peppers, stemmed, seeded, and cut into ¼-inch pieces

4 garlic cloves, minced

2 teaspoons tomato paste

1 teaspoon ground cumin

1 teaspoon turmeric

Salt and pepper

⅛ teaspoon cayenne pepper

1½ cups jarred piquillo peppers, chopped coarse

1 (14.5-ounce) can diced tomatoes

¼ cup water

2 bay leaves

⅓ cup chopped fresh cilantro

8 large eggs

2 ounces feta cheese, crumbled (½ cup)

1. Heat oil in 12-inch skillet over medium-high heat until shimmering. Add onions and bell peppers and cook until softened and beginning to brown, 8 to 10 minutes. Add garlic, tomato paste, cumin, turmeric, 1½ teaspoons salt, ¼ teaspoon pepper, and cayenne, and cook, stirring frequently, until tomato paste begins to darken, about 3 minutes.

2. Stir in piquillo peppers, tomatoes and their juice, water, and bay leaves and bring to simmer. Reduce heat to medium-low and cook, stirring occasionally, until sauce is slightly thickened, 10 to 15 minutes.

3. Off heat, discard bay leaves and stir in ¼ cup cilantro. Transfer 2 cups sauce to blender and process until smooth, about 60 seconds. Return puree to skillet and bring sauce to simmer over medium-low heat.

4. Off heat, make 4 shallow indentations (about 2 inches wide) in surface of sauce using back of spoon. Crack 2 eggs into each indentation and season eggs with salt and pepper. Cover and cook over medium-low heat until egg whites are just set and yolks are still runny, 5 to 10 minutes. Sprinkle with feta and remaining cilantro and serve.

# huevos rancheros

*why this recipe works* Huevos rancheros is a perennial crowd pleaser, with its spicy, smoky tomato-chile sauce, runny fried eggs, soft tortillas, and flavorful fixings like diced avocado and melted cheese, but tackling its many components can be challenging. To streamline this brunch staple while keeping its deep flavors intact, we prepared all of its elements in a sheet pan. To start, we built a strong tomato sauce by roasting canned diced tomatoes, onion, and chiles, concentrating their flavors and imparting some tasty char. Stirring in the juice drained from the tomatoes created a saucy, bright-flavored bed for our eggs. After sprinkling on pepper Jack cheese, we created eight wells in the sauce and cracked in the eggs. Stacking a second pan underneath the sheet offered just enough insulation against overcooking, promising perfectly runny yolks nestled in our rich, brick-red sauce. As soon as the eggs were just set, we topped off our one-pan huevos rancheros with cool diced avocado, sliced scallions, and minced cilantro and tucked the eggs and sauce into tortillas softened in the oven. We like our eggs slightly runny; if you prefer well-done eggs, cook them to the end of the time range in step 4. Use heavyweight rimmed baking sheets; flimsy sheets will warp. Serve with hot sauce.

*serves 4*
*total time: 1 hour 15 minutes*

2 (28-ounce) cans diced tomatoes

1 tablespoon packed brown sugar

1 tablespoon lime juice

1 onion, chopped

½ cup canned chopped green chiles

¼ cup extra-virgin olive oil

3 tablespoons chili powder

4 garlic cloves, sliced thin

Salt and pepper

8 (6-inch) corn tortillas

4 ounces pepper Jack cheese, shredded (1 cup)

8 large eggs

1 avocado, halved, pitted, and diced

2 scallions, sliced thin

¼ cup minced fresh cilantro

1. Adjust oven racks to lowest and middle positions and heat oven to 500 degrees. Drain tomatoes in fine-mesh strainer set over bowl, pressing with rubber spatula to extract as much juice as possible. Combine 1¾ cups drained tomato juice, sugar, and lime juice in bowl and set aside; discard extra drained juice.

2. Combine tomatoes, onion, chiles, oil, chili powder, garlic, and ½ teaspoon salt in bowl, then spread mixture out evenly on rimmed baking sheet. Wrap tortillas in aluminum foil and place on lower rack. Place sheet with tomato mixture on upper rack and roast until charred in spots, 35 to 40 minutes, stirring and redistributing into even layer halfway through roasting.

3. Remove sheet from oven and place inside second rimmed baking sheet. Carefully stir reserved tomato juice mixture into roasted vegetables, season with salt and pepper to taste, and spread into even layer. Sprinkle pepper Jack over top and, using back of spoon, hollow out eight 3-inch-wide holes in mixture. Crack 1 egg into each hole and season with salt and pepper.

4. Bake until whites are just beginning to set but still have some movement when sheet is shaken, 7 to 8 minutes for slightly runny yolks or 9 to 10 minutes for soft-cooked yolks, rotating sheet halfway through baking.

5. Remove sheet from oven and top with avocado, scallions, and cilantro. To serve, slide spatula underneath eggs and sauce and gently transfer to warm tortillas.

# pancakes, waffles, and french toast

# classic buttermilk pancakes

*why this recipe works* A stack of fluffy, golden pancakes is the perfect starting place for a standout brunch, delivering piping hot cakes with distinct sweet tang and an open, airy texture. Buttermilk was a must—it contributed to the pancakes' flavor and, with some leavening help from small amounts of baking powder and baking soda, it also created pancakes with better texture—but we craved even more tang, so we whisked in some sour cream for a concentrated boost. To keep our pancakes as light and fluffy as possible, we avoided overmixing the batter, which would overdevelop the gluten and make the pancakes tough. After a brief rest to relax the gluten, we portioned the batter into a hot, lightly oiled skillet. From there, our cakes needed just a few minutes per side to turn beautifully golden brown. To ensure all our guests would enjoy fresh, hot pancakes, we kept the cakes warm while we finished the remaining batches by transferring the finished pancakes to a warm oven until it was time to serve. Getting the skillet hot enough before making the pancakes is key. An electric griddle set to 350 degrees can also be used to cook the pancakes.

*makes sixteen 4-inch pancakes*
*total time: 30 minutes*

2 cups (10 ounces) all-purpose flour

2 tablespoons sugar

1 teaspoon baking powder

½ teaspoon baking soda

½ teaspoon salt

2 cups buttermilk

¼ cup sour cream

2 large eggs

3 tablespoons unsalted butter, melted and cooled slightly

1–2 teaspoons vegetable oil

**1.** Adjust oven rack to middle position and heat oven to 200 degrees. Set wire rack in rimmed baking sheet and place in oven.

**2.** Whisk flour, sugar, baking powder, baking soda, and salt together in large bowl. In separate bowl, whisk buttermilk, sour cream, eggs, and melted butter together. Make well in center of dry ingredients and pour in wet ingredients; gently stir until just combined (batter should be lumpy with few streaks of flour). Do not overmix. Let batter sit 10 minutes before cooking.

**3.** Heat 1 teaspoon oil in 12-inch nonstick skillet over medium heat until shimmering. Using paper towels, carefully wipe out oil, leaving thin film on bottom and sides of pan.

**4.** Using ¼-cup measure, portion batter into pan in 4 places. Cook until edges are set, first side is golden brown, and bubbles on surface are just beginning to break, 2 to 3 minutes. Using thin, wide spatula, flip pancakes and continue to cook until second side is golden brown, 1 to 2 minutes. Transfer to wire rack in oven and repeat with remaining batter, using remaining oil as necessary. Serve.

## variations

blueberry buttermilk pancakes
Sprinkle 1 tablespoon fresh blueberries over each pancake before flipping. (If using frozen berries, thaw and rinse berries and spread them out on paper towels to dry.)

graham buttermilk pancakes
Substitute 1 cup graham cracker crumbs plus 2 tablespoons cornmeal for 1 cup flour.

# fluffy cornmeal pancakes

*why this recipe works* Cornmeal pancakes are at their best when their texture is light and fluffy and their flavor boasts the unmistakable taste of sweet, toasty corn, and this recipe achieves both in spades. Coarsely ground cornmeal can yield overly sandy pancakes, and it lacks the gluten necessary to support a fluffy internal structure, but by microwaving the cornmeal with tangy buttermilk and rich butter and giving the mixture a few minutes' rest, we were able to soften its texture for a grit-free batter. A second rest after stirring the thickened, porridge-like mixture into the remaining ingredients gave the baking soda and buttermilk time to react for batter that rose high in the pan. With that, we were rewarded with fluffy, sunshine-yellow pancakes bursting with sweet corn flavor. Our favorite cornmeal is Arrowhead Mills Organic Yellow Cornmeal. An electric griddle set to 350 degrees can also be used to cook the pancakes.

*makes fifteen 4-inch pancakes*
*total time: 45 minutes*

1¾ cups buttermilk

1¼ cups (6¼ ounces) cornmeal

2 tablespoons unsalted butter, cut into ¼-inch pieces

¾ cup (3¾ ounces) all-purpose flour

2 tablespoons sugar

1¾ teaspoons baking powder

½ teaspoon baking soda

½ teaspoon salt

2 large eggs

2½ teaspoons vegetable oil

1. Adjust oven rack to middle position and heat oven to 200 degrees. Set wire rack in rimmed baking sheet and place in oven.

2. Whisk 1¼ cups buttermilk and cornmeal together in medium bowl. Stir in butter, cover, and microwave until slightly thickened around edges, about 90 seconds, stirring once halfway through cooking. Let sit, covered, for 5 minutes.

3. Whisk flour, sugar, baking powder, baking soda, and salt in large bowl. Beat eggs and remaining ½ cup buttermilk together in 1-cup liquid measuring cup. Whisk egg mixture into cornmeal mixture. Whisk cornmeal mixture into flour mixture. Let sit for 10 minutes.

4. Heat ½ teaspoon oil in 12-inch nonstick skillet over medium-low heat until shimmering. Using paper towels, carefully wipe out oil, leaving thin film on bottom and sides of pan. Using level ¼-cup measure, portion batter into pan in 3 places. Cook until edges are set and bubbles begin to form on tops of pancakes, about 90 seconds. Using thin, wide spatula, flip pancakes and continue to cook until second side is golden brown, about 2 minutes longer. Transfer to prepared wire rack in oven and cover loosely with aluminum foil. Repeat with remaining oil and batter. Serve.

# syrups and other toppings

Adding a sweet flourish to a stack of waffles or a humble Dutch baby gives your brunch a professional finish. Here are some quick and easy ways to add panache to your brunch sweets.

## butter-pecan maple syrup
*makes about 2 cups*

1½ cups maple syrup

2 tablespoons unsalted butter

½ cup pecans, toasted and chopped

¼ teaspoon vanilla extract

Pinch salt

Simmer all ingredients in small saucepan over medium-low heat until slightly thickened, about 5 minutes.

## berry maple syrup
*makes about 1¾ cups*

½ cup frozen blueberries, strawberries, or raspberries

1½ cups maple syrup

¼ teaspoon grated lemon zest

Pinch salt

Mash berries in small saucepan over medium heat until moisture has evaporated, about 5 minutes. Whisk in remaining ingredients, reduce heat to medium-low, and cook until slightly thickened, 5 to 7 minutes.

## apple-cinnamon maple syrup
*makes about 1¾ cups*

1½ cups maple syrup

⅓ cup apple jelly

¼ teaspoon ground cinnamon

Pinch salt

Simmer all ingredients in small saucepan over medium-low heat until slightly thickened, 5 to 7 minutes.

## whipped cream
*makes about 1 cup*
*For lightly sweetened whipped cream, reduce the sugar to ¾ teaspoon. For the best results, chill the bowl and beaters in the freezer for 20 minutes before whipping the cream.*

½ cup heavy cream, chilled

1½ teaspoons sugar

½ teaspoon vanilla extract

Using hand mixer, whip cream, sugar, and vanilla on medium-low speed until foamy, about 1 minute. Increase speed to high and whip until soft peaks form, 1 to 3 minutes.

**to make ahead**
Whipped cream can be refrigerated in fine-mesh strainer set over small bowl and covered with plastic wrap for up to 8 hours.

## maple butter
*makes ¼ cup*

4 tablespoons unsalted butter, softened

1 tablespoon maple syrup

¼ teaspoon salt

Whisk butter, maple syrup, and salt in bowl until combined.

**to make ahead**
Maple butter can be refrigerated, covered, for up to 1 week.

## syrup dispensers
Keeping your syrup in a dispenser reduces mess when pouring the sweet stuff over pancakes, waffles, and French toast. Of the models we tested, the **American Metalcraft Beehive Syrup Dispenser, 6 oz** ($7.80) proved easiest to fill and clean, and its spring-loaded spout cover made pouring neat and precise.

## simple fruit toppings
*makes 2½ to 3 cups*

Combine all ingredients in bowl and microwave until fruits are softened but not mushy and juices are slightly thickened, 4 to 6 minutes, stirring once halfway through microwaving. Remove from microwave and stir, adding any fresh berries if called for. Serve.

### apple-cranberry topping

3 Golden Delicious apples, peeled, halved, cored, and cut into ¼-inch pieces

¼ cup dried cranberries

1 tablespoon sugar

1 teaspoon cornstarch

Pinch salt

Pinch ground nutmeg

### pear-blackberry topping

3 ripe pears, peeled, halved, cored, and cut into ¼-inch pieces

1 tablespoon sugar

1 teaspoon cornstarch

Pinch salt

Pinch ground cardamom

1 cup (5 ounces) blackberries, berries more than 1 inch long cut in half crosswise

### plum-apricot topping

1½ pounds plums, halved, pitted, and cut into ¼-inch pieces

¼ cup dried apricots, chopped coarse

1 tablespoon sugar

1 teaspoon cornstarch

Pinch salt

Pinch ground cinnamon

# lemon ricotta pancakes

*why this recipe works* These remarkably fluffy ricotta pancakes are perfect for a sophisticated brunch. The secret to their light and airy texture? Some clever leavening. Despite the addition of a full cup of heavy, wet ricotta cheese, the combination of baking soda and whipped egg whites gave our enriched cakes incredible rising power. The baking soda also boosted browning for gorgeously browned pancakes. Baking soda requires an acid to react, so we added lemon juice and quickly discovered that its bright, fresh flavor was the perfect complement to the creamy ricotta; we then added a teaspoon of lemon zest to double down on the citrus flavor we loved without adding any additional moisture to the batter. A touch of vanilla extract brought depth and subtle sweetness to these rich yet airy cakes. An electric griddle set at 325 degrees can also be used to cook the pancakes. We prefer the flavor of whole-milk ricotta, but part-skim will work, too; avoid nonfat ricotta. Serve with honey, confectioners' sugar, or one of our fruit toppings (page 39).

*makes twelve 4-inch pancakes*
*total time: 45 minutes*

⅔ cup (3⅓ ounces)
all-purpose flour

½ teaspoon baking soda

½ teaspoon salt

8 ounces (1 cup) whole-milk
ricotta cheese

2 large eggs, separated,
plus 2 large whites

⅓ cup whole milk

1 teaspoon grated lemon zest
plus 4 teaspoons juice

½ teaspoon vanilla extract

2 tablespoons unsalted
butter, melted

¼ cup (1¾ ounces) sugar

1–2 teaspoons vegetable oil

1. Adjust oven rack to middle position and heat oven to 200 degrees. Set wire rack in rimmed baking sheet and place in oven.

2. Whisk flour, baking soda, and salt together in medium bowl and make well in center. Add ricotta, egg yolks, milk, lemon zest and juice, and vanilla and whisk until just combined. Gently stir in melted butter.

3. Using stand mixer fitted with whisk, whip egg whites on medium-low speed until foamy, about 1 minute. Increase speed to medium-high and whip whites to soft, billowy mounds, about 1 minute. Gradually add sugar and whip until glossy, soft peaks form, 1 to 2 minutes. Transfer one-third of whipped egg whites to batter and whisk gently until mixture is lightened. Using rubber spatula, gently fold remaining egg whites into batter.

4. Heat 1 teaspoon oil in 12-inch nonstick skillet over medium heat until shimmering. Using paper towels, wipe out oil, leaving thin film on bottom and sides of pan. Using ¼-cup measure, portion batter into pan in 3 places, leaving 2 inches between portions. Gently spread each portion into 4-inch round. Cook until edges are set and first side is deep golden brown, 2 to 3 minutes. Using thin, wide spatula, flip pancakes and continue to cook until second side is golden brown, 2 to 3 minutes longer. Transfer to prepared wire rack in oven. Repeat with remaining batter, using remaining oil as needed. Serve.

# dutch baby

*why this recipe works* This crisp, custardy pancake rises spectacularly in the oven and then falls in the center within minutes of leaving it, resulting in a bowl-shaped brunch treat perfect for sharing. The success of this recipe resides in two secret weapons: a ripping-hot skillet and some skim milk. Working with a 12-inch skillet meant there'd be enough Dutch baby to go around; plus, its gently sloped sides would allow an even, supported lift. Brushing the pan with oil and preheating it in the oven jump-started the pancake's dramatic rise on contact. Fats tend to make baked goods tender rather than crisp, so we swapped whole milk for lean skim milk in our batter. A touch of vanilla and lemon zest more than compensated for the decreased richness. Finally, for even more crackle, we replaced some of the flour with cornstarch. After carefully combining the wet and dry ingredients, we poured the batter into the hot skillet and baked it, the steam from the milk, eggs, and butter causing our Dutch baby to quickly inflate and rise above the sides of the pan. Finished with a generous dusting of confectioners' sugar and a squeeze of lemon, our golden-brown Dutch baby was a crisp and custardy bundle of joy. You can use whole or 2 percent low-fat milk instead of skim, but the Dutch baby won't be as crisp. Serve with maple syrup or with an assortment of berries and Whipped Cream (page 38), if desired.

*serves 4*
*total time: 45 minutes*

2 tablespoons vegetable oil

1 cup (5 ounces) all-purpose flour

¼ cup (1 ounce) cornstarch

2 teaspoons grated lemon zest plus 2 tablespoons juice

1 teaspoon salt

3 large eggs

1¼ cups skim milk

1 tablespoon unsalted butter, melted and cooled

1 teaspoon vanilla extract

3 tablespoons confectioners' sugar

**1.** Adjust oven rack to middle position and heat oven to 450 degrees. Brush surface and sides of 12-inch skillet with oil. Place skillet on oven rack and heat until oil is shimmering, about 10 minutes.

**2.** Meanwhile, combine flour, cornstarch, lemon zest, and salt in large bowl. Whisk eggs in second bowl until frothy and light, about 1 minute. Whisk milk, melted butter, and vanilla into eggs until incorporated. Whisk one-third of milk mixture into flour mixture until no lumps remain, then slowly whisk in remaining milk mixture until smooth.

**3.** Carefully pour batter into heated skillet and bake until edges of Dutch baby are deep golden brown and crisp, about 20 minutes. Transfer skillet to wire rack and sprinkle Dutch baby with lemon juice and sugar. Cut into wedges and serve.

# yeasted waffles

*why this recipe works* Raised waffles are barely on the current culinary radar, and that's a shame. At once creamy and airy, tangy and salty, refined and complex, this recipe blows the competition out of the water, and because the batter must be made ahead of time, it makes for a truly fuss-free brunch. Most yeasted waffles call for the batter (sans eggs) to rise overnight unrefrigerated, but we discovered that preparing the batter with eggs and slowing its fermentation in the refrigerator yielded waffles with deeper, more nuanced flavor. A teaspoon and a half of instant yeast imparted plenty of tang and just the right open texture, and a touch of vanilla and salt helped balance out the flavor. A whole stick of melted butter and some milk rounded out the richness and tender texture, the butter encouraging a golden, extra-crisp exterior. With our risen batter at the ready, all we had to do in the morning was heat up the waffle iron. While the waffles can be eaten as soon as they are removed from the iron, they will have a crispier exterior if rested in a warm oven for 10 minutes. (This method also makes it possible to serve everyone at the same time.) The batter must sit in the refrigerator for at least 12 hours. The number of waffles this recipe yields will depend on the size and style of your waffle maker. Our favorite waffle maker is the Cuisinart Double Belgian Waffle Maker.

*makes six 7-inch waffles*
*total time: 45 minutes*
*(plus 12 hours chilling time)*

1¾ cups milk

8 tablespoons unsalted butter, cut into 8 pieces

2 cups (10 ounces) all-purpose flour

1 tablespoon sugar

1½ teaspoons instant or rapid-rise yeast

1 teaspoon salt

2 large eggs

1 teaspoon vanilla extract

1. Heat milk and butter in small saucepan over medium-low heat until butter is melted, 3 to 5 minutes. Let mixture cool until warm to touch.

2. Whisk flour, sugar, yeast, and salt together in large bowl. In separate bowl, whisk eggs and vanilla together. Gradually whisk warm milk mixture into flour mixture until smooth, then whisk in egg mixture. Scrape down bowl with rubber spatula, cover tightly with plastic wrap, and refrigerate for at least 12 hours.

3. Adjust oven rack to middle position and heat oven to 200 degrees. Set wire rack in rimmed baking sheet and place in oven. Heat waffle iron according to manufacturer's instructions. Remove batter from refrigerator when waffle iron is hot (batter will be foamy and doubled in size). Whisk batter to recombine (batter will deflate).

4. Spray preheated waffle iron with vegetable oil spray. Add ⅔ cup batter to waffle iron and cook according to manufacturer's instructions until crisp, firm, and golden, 4 to 6 minutes. Transfer to wire rack in oven. Repeat with remaining batter. Serve.

**variation**

blueberry yeasted waffles
*Frozen wild blueberries, which are smaller, work best here. Larger blueberries release too much juice.*

After removing waffle batter from refrigerator in step 3, gently fold 1½ cups frozen blueberries into batter.

**to make ahead**
Waffle batter, prepared through step 2, can be refrigerated for up to 24 hours.

# ham and cheese waffles

*why this recipe works* These sweet-meets-savory waffles are undeniably appealing, boasting salty bites of deli ham and rich swirls of cheese tucked into a crisp, buttery crust. To infuse these simple waffles with enough deep flavor to reinforce the cheese's bright tang, we boosted a buttermilk batter with a touch of dry mustard. Equal amounts of finely chopped deli ham and shredded cheddar folded into the batter promised salty, savory goodness in every nook and cranny, and baking powder and plenty of butter ensured a crisp, rich, browned exterior. Served piping hot topped off with a runny fried egg or a drizzle of maple syrup, these indulgent waffles were perfect brunch fare. The number of waffles this recipe yields will depend on the size and style of your waffle maker. Our favorite waffle maker is the Cuisinart Double Belgian Waffle Maker.

*makes four 7-inch waffles*
*total time: 45 minutes*

2 cups (10 ounces) all-purpose flour

1 tablespoon sugar

1 teaspoon baking powder

1 teaspoon salt

⅛ teaspoon dry mustard

1¾ cups buttermilk

4 tablespoons unsalted butter, melted and cooled

1 large egg

3 ounces sliced deli ham, chopped fine

3 ounces cheddar, Gruyère, or fontina cheese, shredded (¾ cup)

1. Adjust rack to middle position and heat oven to 200 degrees. Set wire rack in rimmed baking sheet and place in oven.

2. Whisk flour, sugar, baking powder, salt, and mustard together in large bowl. In separate bowl, whisk buttermilk, melted butter, and egg together. Make a well in center of flour mixture, pour buttermilk mixture into well, and gently whisk together until just incorporated with few lumps remaining (do not overmix). Gently fold in ham and cheddar with rubber spatula.

3. Meanwhile, heat waffle iron according to manufacturer's instructions and spray with vegetable oil spray. Add ⅔ cup batter to waffle iron and cook according to manufacturer's instructions until golden brown, about 3½ minutes. Transfer to wire rack in oven. Repeat with remaining batter. Serve.

# french toast

*why this recipe works*  This foolproof French toast recipe guarantees crisp, custardy slices by keeping things simple. Stale bread is standard, but we got better (and more efficient) results from oven-dried slices. For the batter, we beat milk, egg yolks, and melted butter for an indulgent coating; brown sugar, vanilla, and cinnamon added warm, sweet flavors. After soaking the slices in batter, we cooked them over medium-low to gradually impart a golden-brown crust. Prevent the butter from clumping by warming the milk in the microwave or a saucepan until warm to the touch (about 80 degrees). An electric griddle set at 350 degrees can also be used to cook the French toast, but it may take an extra 2 to 3 minutes per side. Cook the slices all at once using the entire amount of butter for cooking.

*serves 4*
*total time: 1 hour*

8 large slices hearty white sandwich bread or challah

1½ cups whole milk, warmed

3 large egg yolks

3 tablespoons packed light brown sugar

2 tablespoons unsalted butter, melted, plus 2 tablespoons unsalted butter

1 tablespoon vanilla extract

½ teaspoon ground cinnamon

¼ teaspoon salt

**1.** Adjust oven rack to middle position and heat oven to 300 degrees. Place bread on wire rack set in rimmed baking sheet. Bake bread until almost dry throughout (center should remain slightly moist), about 15 minutes, flipping slices halfway through baking. Remove bread from rack and let cool for 5 minutes. Return baking sheet with wire rack to oven and reduce temperature to 200 degrees.

**2.** Whisk milk, egg yolks, sugar, 2 tablespoons melted butter, vanilla, cinnamon, and salt together in bowl. Transfer mixture to 13 by 9-inch baking pan.

**3.** Soak bread in milk mixture until saturated but not falling apart, 20 seconds per side. Using firm slotted spatula, remove bread from milk mixture, 1 piece at a time, allowing excess milk mixture to drip back into pan, and transfer to clean rimmed baking sheet in single layer.

**4.** Melt ½ tablespoon butter in 12-inch skillet over medium-low heat. Using slotted spatula, transfer 2 slices soaked bread to skillet and cook until golden on first side, 3 to 4 minutes. Flip and continue to cook until second side is golden, 3 to 4 minutes. Transfer toast to wire rack in oven. Wipe out skillet with paper towels and repeat with remaining bread, 2 pieces at a time, adding ½ tablespoon butter to skillet for each batch. Serve.

## variations

### extra-crisp french toast
Pulse 1 slice hearty white sandwich bread or challah, torn into 1-inch pieces, 1 tablespoon packed light brown sugar, and ¼ teaspoon ground cinnamon in food processor until finely ground, 8 to 12 pulses (you should have about ½ cup). Sprinkle 1 tablespoon processed crumb mixture over 1 side of each slice of soaked bread. Cook as directed, starting with crumb mixture side down.

### almond-crusted french toast
Pulse ½ cup slivered almonds and 1 tablespoon packed light brown sugar in food processor until coarsely ground, 12 to 15 pulses (you should have about ½ cup). Add 1 tablespoon triple sec and 1 teaspoon grated orange zest to milk mixture in step 2. Sprinkle 1 tablespoon processed nut mixture over 1 side of each slice of soaked bread. Cook as directed, starting with nut mixture side down.

### pecan-rum french toast
Substitute 8 large slices cinnamon-raisin bread for hearty white sandwich bread. Pulse ½ cup pecans, 1 tablespoon packed light brown sugar, and ¼ teaspoon ground cinnamon in food processor until coarsely ground, 12 to 15 pulses (you should have about ½ cup). Add 2 teaspoons dark rum to milk mixture in step 2. Sprinkle 1 tablespoon processed nut mixture over 1 side of each slice of soaked bread. Cook as directed, starting with nut mixture side down.

# crêpes with sugar and lemon

*why this recipe works* Crêpes have a reputation for being temperamental, but our simple method makes this specialty pancake accessible without sacrificing its delicate texture and signature richness. We discovered that we could cook authentic crêpes in a standard 12-inch nonstick skillet—no special equipment necessary. What did matter: heating the pan properly (over low heat for at least 10 minutes), using the right amount of batter (we settled on ¼ cup), and flipping the crêpe precisely when the edges appeared dry, matte, and lacy. To transform our perfectly cooked crêpes into decadent brunch sweets, we whipped up a few tempting fillings, starting with the simple classic of sugar and lemon. Crêpes give off steam as they cook, but if at any point the skillet begins to smoke, remove it from the heat immediately and turn down the heat. Stacking the crêpes on a wire rack allows excess steam to escape so they won't stick together. To allow for practice, the recipe yields 10 crêpes; only eight are needed for the filling.

*makes eight 12-inch crêpes*
*total time: 30 minutes*

½ teaspoon vegetable oil

1 cup (5 ounces)
all-purpose flour

3 tablespoons sugar

¼ teaspoon salt

1½ cups whole milk

3 large eggs

2 tablespoons unsalted butter,
melted and cooled

Lemon wedges

1. Heat oil in 12-inch nonstick skillet over low heat for at least 10 minutes.

2. Meanwhile, whisk flour, 1 teaspoon sugar, and salt together in medium bowl. Whisk milk and eggs together in separate bowl. Add half of milk mixture to flour mixture and whisk until smooth. Add melted butter and whisk until incorporated. Whisk in remaining milk mixture until smooth.

3. Wipe out skillet with paper towels, leaving thin film of oil on bottom and sides of pan. Increase heat to medium and let skillet heat for 1 minute. After 1 minute, test heat of skillet by placing 1 teaspoon batter in center of pan and cooking for 20 seconds. If mini crêpe is golden brown on bottom, skillet is properly heated; if it is too light or too dark, adjust heat accordingly and retest.

4. Pour ¼ cup batter into far side of pan and tilt and shake gently until batter evenly covers bottom of pan. Cook crêpe without moving it until top surface is dry and edges are starting to brown, about 25 seconds. Using heat-resistant rubber spatula, loosen crêpe from side of pan. Gently slide spatula underneath edge of crêpe, grasp edge with your fingertips, and flip crêpe. Cook until second side is lightly spotted, about 20 seconds. Transfer cooked crêpe, spotted side up, to wire rack. Return pan to heat and heat for 10 seconds before repeating with remaining batter. As crêpes are done, stack on wire rack.

5. Transfer stack of crêpes to large plate and invert second plate over crêpes. Microwave until crêpes are warm, 30 to 45 seconds (45 to 60 seconds if crêpes have cooled completely). Remove top plate and wipe dry with paper towel. Sprinkle half of top crêpe with 1 teaspoon sugar. Fold unsugared bottom half over sugared half, then fold in half again. Transfer sugared crêpe to second plate. Repeat with remaining crêpes. Serve immediately with lemon wedges.

### variations

**crêpes with bananas and nutella**
Omit 8 teaspoons sugar for sprinkling and lemon wedges. Spread 2 teaspoons Nutella over half of each crêpe, then evenly arrange eight to ten ¼-inch-thick banana slices over Nutella. Fold crêpes as directed. Serve immediately.

**crêpes with chocolate and orange**
Omit 8 teaspoons sugar for sprinkling and lemon wedges. Using your fingertips, rub 1 teaspoon finely grated orange zest into ¼ cup sugar. Stir in 2 ounces finely grated bittersweet chocolate. Sprinkle 1½ tablespoons chocolate-orange mixture over half of each crêpe. Fold crêpes as directed. Serve immediately.

# cheese blintzes with raspberry sauce

*why this recipe works* These blintzes are blissful brunch fare. We boosted the ricotta filling with cream cheese and confectioners' sugar, folded the sweet cheese into each crêpe, and seared the blintzes in a skillet. A quick raspberry sauce offered a sweet finish. The recipe yields 15 crêpes; only 12 are needed for the filling. If the batter doesn't stick to the skillet when swirling, the skillet is too greased and/or not hot enough. Heat the skillet 10 seconds longer and try again. Do not thaw the frozen raspberries.

*makes 12 blintzes*
*total time: 1 hour 30 minutes*

*filling*
11 ounces (1¼ cups plus 2 tablespoons) whole-milk ricotta cheese

½ cup (2 ounces) confectioners' sugar

1 ounce cream cheese, softened

¼ teaspoon salt

*sauce*
10 ounces (2 cups) frozen raspberries

¼ cup (1¾ ounces) granulated sugar

¼ teaspoon salt

*crêpes*
2 cups (10 ounces) all-purpose flour

2 teaspoons granulated sugar

½ teaspoon salt

3 cups whole milk

4 large eggs

4 tablespoons unsalted butter, melted and cooled, plus 4 tablespoons unsalted butter

**1. for the filling** Whisk all ingredients in bowl until no lumps of cream cheese remain. Refrigerate until ready to use.

**2. for the sauce** Combine raspberries, sugar, and salt in small saucepan. Cook over medium heat, stirring occasionally, until slightly thickened, 8 to 10 minutes.

**3. for the crêpes** Whisk flour, sugar, and salt together in medium bowl. Whisk milk and eggs together in separate bowl. Add half of milk mixture to flour mixture and whisk until smooth. Whisk in 3 tablespoons melted butter until incorporated. Whisk in remaining milk mixture until smooth.

**4.** Brush bottom of 12-inch non-stick skillet lightly with some of remaining 1 tablespoon melted butter and heat skillet over medium heat until hot, about 2 minutes. Add ⅓ cup batter to center of skillet and simultaneously lift and rotate skillet in circular motion to swirl batter, allowing batter to run and fully cover bottom of skillet. Cook crêpe until edges look dry and start to curl and bottom of crêpe is light golden, about 1 minute. Using rubber spatula, lift edge of crêpe and slide it onto plate. Repeat with remaining batter, stacking crêpes and brushing skillet with melted butter every other time. (Adjust burner between medium-low and medium heat as needed toward end of crêpe-making process.)

**5.** Working with 1 crêpe at a time, spoon 2 tablespoons filling onto crêpe about 2 inches from bottom edge and spread into 4-inch line.

Fold bottom edge of crêpe over filling, then fold sides of crêpe over filling. Gently roll crêpe into tidy package about 4 inches long and 2 inches wide. Repeat with remaining crêpes and filling.

**6.** Melt 2 tablespoons butter in now-empty skillet over medium heat. Add half of blintzes, seam sides down, and cook until golden brown, 2 to 4 minutes, gently moving blintzes in skillet as needed for even browning. Using spatula, gently flip blintzes and continue to cook until golden brown on second side, 2 to 4 minutes longer. Transfer blintzes to platter, seam sides down, and wipe skillet clean with paper towels. Repeat with remaining 2 tablespoons butter and remaining blintzes. Serve with raspberry sauce.

**to make ahead**
Filling, sauce, and batter can be refrigerated for up to 2 days; rewhisk batter before proceeding with recipe. Blintzes can be refrigerated for up to 24 hours or frozen for up to 1 month following step 5. Freeze blintzes on a rimmed baking sheet then store in a zipper-lock bag. When ready to cook, do not thaw blintzes, but reduce heat in step 6 to medium-low and cook blintzes, covered, until golden brown, 6 to 9 minutes per side.

savory
mains

# cheese soufflé

*why this recipe works* With bold cheese flavor, good stature, and a light but not-too-airy texture, this cheese soufflé pairs well with a crisp salad or side of fruit, making for a simple but stately brunch. To amplify the cheese flavor without weighing down the soufflé, we added lightweight but flavorful grated Parmesan cheese to the traditional Gruyère (and even sprinkled some into the greased soufflé dish) and reduced the amount of butter and flour in the base. Filling the soufflé dish to an inch below the rim allowed ample room for the soufflé to rise high. Some recipes incorporate a lot of air into the soufflé by delicately whisking the cheese into the eggs, but this produces an overly light, foamy texture. By instead stirring the savory cheese sauce right into the eggs, we achieved a billowy soufflé that was still substantial enough to serve as a main course. Baked until its center reached 170 degrees, our rich, cheesy, high-flying soufflé boasted a luscious creamy center beneath its lightly bronzed edges. Comté, sharp cheddar, or gouda cheese can be substituted for the Gruyère. To prevent the soufflé from overflowing the soufflé dish, leave at least 1 inch of space between the top of the batter and the rim of the dish; any excess batter should be discarded. The most foolproof way to test for doneness is with an instant-read thermometer. To judge doneness without an instant-read thermometer, use two large spoons to pry open the soufflé so that you can peer inside it; the center should appear thick and creamy but not soupy.

*serves 4 to 6*
*total time: 1 hour*

1 ounce Parmesan cheese, grated (½ cup)

¼ cup (1¼ ounces) all-purpose flour

¼ teaspoon paprika

¼ teaspoon salt

⅛ teaspoon cayenne pepper

⅛ teaspoon white pepper

Pinch ground nutmeg

4 tablespoons unsalted butter

1⅓ cups whole milk

6 ounces Gruyère cheese, shredded (1½ cups)

6 large eggs, separated

2 teaspoons minced fresh parsley

¼ teaspoon cream of tartar

**1.** Adjust oven rack to middle position and heat oven to 350 degrees. Spray 8-inch round (2-quart) soufflé dish with vegetable oil spray, then sprinkle with 2 tablespoons Parmesan.

**2.** Whisk flour, paprika, salt, cayenne, white pepper, and nutmeg together in bowl. Melt butter in small saucepan over medium heat. Stir in flour mixture and cook for 1 minute. Slowly whisk in milk and bring to simmer. Cook, whisking constantly, until mixture is thickened and smooth, about 1 minute. Remove pan from heat and whisk in Gruyère and 5 tablespoons Parmesan until melted and smooth. Let cool for 10 minutes, then whisk in egg yolks and 1½ teaspoons parsley.

**3.** Using stand mixer fitted with whisk attachment, whip egg whites and cream of tartar on medium-low speed until foamy, about 1 minute. Increase speed to medium-high and whip until stiff peaks form, 3 to 4 minutes. Add cheese mixture and continue to whip until fully combined, about 15 seconds longer.

**4.** Pour mixture into prepared dish and sprinkle with remaining 1 tablespoon Parmesan. Bake until risen above rim, top is deep golden brown, and interior registers 170 degrees, 30 to 35 minutes. Sprinkle with remaining ½ teaspoon parsley and serve immediately.

# breakfast pizza

*why this recipe works* Putting an egg on pizza creates an easy, unexpected upgrade to brunch, and this recipe delivers a supersatisfying pie thanks to its tasty toppings: crisp bacon, melted cheese, and perfectly runny eggs. We started by crisping strips of bacon in a sheet pan, chopping it up for use as a topping and then saving some of its smoky rendered fat to grease the baking sheet. In order to achieve a flavorful, golden-brown crust without overcooking the eggs, we parbaked the crust on its own for 5 minutes. A layer of cottage cheese, seasoned with oregano, cayenne, and more bacon fat, along with a sprinkling of shredded mozzarella, grated Parmesan, and crisp bacon, gave our pie plenty of richness and flavor. We formed six wells in the toppings to neatly contain the eggs as they cooked. With a few more minutes in the oven, our perfect brunch-ready pizza was ready to serve. Small-curd cottage cheese is sometimes labeled "country style." Room-temperature dough is much easier to shape than cold dough, so pull it from the fridge about 1 hour before you start cooking.

*serves 6*
*total time: 1 hour 15 minutes*

6 slices bacon

8 ounces mozzarella cheese, shredded (2 cups)

1 ounce Parmesan cheese, grated (½ cup)

4 ounces (½ cup) small-curd cottage cheese

¼ teaspoon dried oregano

Salt and pepper

Pinch cayenne pepper

1 pound store-bought pizza dough, room temperature

1 tablespoon extra-virgin olive oil

6 large eggs

2 scallions, sliced thin

1. Adjust oven racks to middle and lowest positions and heat oven to 400 degrees. Place bacon in single layer on rimmed baking sheet and cook on upper rack until crisp, about 15 minutes, rotating sheet halfway through baking. Transfer bacon to paper towel–lined plate, let cool slightly, then crumble. Transfer rendered bacon fat to small bowl and reserve. Let sheet cool to room temperature, about 10 minutes.

2. Increase oven temperature to 500 degrees. Combine mozzarella and Parmesan in bowl. In separate bowl, combine cottage cheese, oregano, ¼ teaspoon pepper, cayenne, and 1 tablespoon reserved bacon fat. Brush 1 tablespoon bacon fat over cooled, now-empty sheet.

3. Press and roll dough into 15 by 11-inch rectangle on lightly floured counter, then transfer to prepared sheet and push to edges of pan. Brush edges of dough with oil.

Bake on lower rack until top of crust appears dry and bottom is just beginning to brown, about 5 minutes.

4. Remove sheet from oven and press on air bubbles with spatula to flatten. Spread cottage cheese mixture evenly over crust, leaving 1-inch border around edge, then sprinkle with crumbled bacon and cheese mixture. Using back of spoon, hollow out six 3-inch-wide holes in cheese. Crack 1 egg into each hole and season each with salt and pepper.

5. Continue to bake pizza until crust is light golden around edges and eggs are just set, 9 to 10 minutes for slightly runny yolks or 11 to 12 minutes for soft-cooked yolks, rotating sheet halfway through baking.

6. Remove sheet from oven. Transfer pizza to cutting board and let cool for 5 minutes. Sprinkle with scallions, slice, and serve.

*why this recipe works* A Monte Cristo is the perfect brunch sandwich, stacking salty, smoky ham, turkey, and cheese between slices of custardy-yet-crisp French toast–like bread. It's simple enough to prepare this sandwich for one, but our recipe yields six salty-sweet stacks at once for a totally streamlined meal. We began by toasting hearty sandwich bread, drying it out so it stayed crisp even when brushed with batter. A mixture of eggs, heavy cream, dry mustard, and cayenne served as our savory, spiced batter, and adding a touch of sugar ensured the bread's surface would crisp and caramelize in the oven. Monte Cristos are always served with a sweet jam for dipping, but to keep our sandwiches' flavors from becoming cloying, we cut strawberry jam with Dijon mustard to offset the sweetness. Spreading some of the jam-Dijon sauce on the bread carried its contrasting flavors into every bite. After we layered all the ham, turkey, and Swiss on the toasted bread and coated the sandwiches with batter, we arranged them on a preheated oiled baking sheet to kick-start their sizzle. Ten minutes in a hot oven (with a flip halfway through for even browning) was all it took to turn out a platter of hot, crisp sandwiches. With a dusting of confectioners' sugar and our jam-mustard sauce on the side, these sweet-and-salty sandwiches were ready for brunch. Trim the slices of meat and cheese as necessary to fit neatly on the bread.

*serves 6*
*total time: 30 minutes*

4 large eggs

¼ cup heavy cream

2 teaspoons sugar

½ teaspoon salt

½ teaspoon dry mustard

⅛ teaspoon cayenne pepper

6 tablespoons strawberry or raspberry jam

2 tablespoons Dijon mustard

12 slices hearty white sandwich bread, lightly toasted

18 thin slices deli Swiss or Gruyère cheese

12 thin slices deli ham

12 thin slices deli turkey

3 tablespoons vegetable oil

Confectioners' sugar

1. Adjust oven rack to upper-middle position and heat oven to 450 degrees. Whisk together eggs, cream, sugar, salt, dry mustard, and cayenne in shallow dish until combined. Stir jam and Dijon mustard together in small bowl.

2. Spread 1 teaspoon jam mixture on 1 side of each slice of toast. Layer slices of cheese, ham, and turkey over jam on 6 slices of toast. Repeat with second layer of cheese, ham, and turkey. Add final layer of cheese and top with remaining toast, with jam side facing cheese. Using your hands, lightly press down on sandwiches.

3. Pour oil into rimmed baking sheet and heat in oven until just smoking, about 7 minutes. Meanwhile, using both hands to hold sandwich, coat each sandwich with egg mixture and transfer to large plate. Transfer sandwiches to preheated baking sheet and bake until golden brown, 8 to 10 minutes, flipping sandwiches halfway through baking. Sprinkle with confectioners' sugar and serve immediately with remaining jam mixture.

# croque monsieurs

*why this recipe works* Think of a croque monsieur as a griddled ham and cheese sandwich's indulgent French cousin. Oozing with nutty Gruyère and salty ham, croque monsieurs are a bistro brunch favorite, and our version streamlines this sandwich's many components for a fuss-free meal. Croque monsieurs are at once crisp and creamy thanks to a quick soak in beaten eggs and a thick layer of bubbly browned béchamel sauce spread onto the top slice. For our version, we nixed the egg dip, instead boosting the béchamel with plenty of shredded Gruyère for a supremely rich sandwich. We prepared the cheesy sauce on the stovetop and then turned our attention to the sandwiches. Rather than cooking each one in a skillet, we decided to take on four croque monsieurs at once by baking them on a sheet pan. Buttering the bottom slice of bread promised some rich browning, and from there we slathered on some mustard and stacked thin slices of deli ham and quick-melting shredded cheese. Topped off with our Gruyère-boosted béchamel and a final helping of shredded cheese and baked in a hot oven, this pan of sandwiches emerged browned and caramelized for a bistro-perfect brunch. We like to use Gruyère, but Comté or Emmentaler can be substituted for it.

*serves 4*
*total time: 30 minutes*

---

**3 tablespoons butter, softened**

**2 tablespoons all-purpose flour**

**1 cup whole milk**

**10 ounces Gruyère cheese, shredded (2½ cups)**

**Salt and pepper**

**8 slices hearty white sandwich bread**

**2 tablespoons Dijon mustard**

**8 thin slices deli ham**

**1.** Adjust oven rack to upper-middle position and heat oven to 475 degrees. Melt 2 tablespoons butter in saucepan over medium heat. Whisk in flour and cook until golden, about 2 minutes. Slowly whisk in milk and simmer until slightly thickened, 3 to 5 minutes. Off heat, stir in ½ cup Gruyère, ¼ teaspoon salt, and ¼ teaspoon pepper. Cover and keep warm.

**2.** Spread remaining butter over 4 slices of bread. Arrange, buttered side down, on rimmed baking sheet. Spread each slice with mustard, then divide ham, 1 cup Gruyère, and ½ cup sauce over mustard-topped slices and top with remaining bread. Top with remaining sauce and Gruyère. Bake until cheese is golden brown and bubbling, 8 to 10 minutes. Serve.

# spicy shrimp skewers with cheesy grits

*why this recipe works* This recipe makes serving the classic Southern brunch of tender spiced shrimp and creamy grits a totally streamlined pursuit thanks to a few skewers and an innovative cooking technique. After readying a generous batch of rich, cheesy grits in a baking dish, we made light work of cooking plenty of shrimp at once by skewering them head to tail and propping the skewers widthwise across the dish of bubbly grits. A chili powder–spiced butter gave the shrimp plenty of pleasant heat. By the time the shrimp had cooked through, our grits were nicely thickened. In lieu of the seasoned sauce we would have gotten from sautéing the shrimp, we pulled together a fragrant mixture of butter, chili powder, and smoky chipotle chile powder to dollop on when serving. Chopped scallions and lime wedges finished the dish with a burst of freshness. The grits' cooking time in step 1 will depend on the brand of grits. You will need eight 12-inch metal or bamboo skewers for this recipe.

*serves 4 to 6*
*total time: 1 hour 30 minutes*

4½ cups chicken broth

1½ cups old-fashioned grits

¾ cup whole milk

3 scallions, white parts minced, green parts sliced thin on bias

2 garlic cloves, minced

Salt and pepper

1½ pounds jumbo shrimp (16 to 20 per pound), peeled and deveined

4 tablespoons unsalted butter, melted

2 teaspoons chili powder

6 ounces sharp cheddar cheese, shredded (1½ cups)

1 teaspoon chipotle chile powder

Lime wedges

1. Adjust oven rack to middle position and heat oven to 350 degrees. Spray 13 by 9-inch baking dish with vegetable oil spray. Combine broth, grits, milk, scallion whites, garlic, and ¼ teaspoon salt in prepared dish, cover tightly with aluminum foil, and bake until grits are tender, 50 minutes to 1¼ hours.

2. Pat shrimp dry with paper towels and toss in bowl with 1 tablespoon melted butter, 1 teaspoon chili powder, ¼ teaspoon salt, and ¼ teaspoon pepper. Working with 1 shrimp at a time, thread tail onto one 12-inch skewer, and head onto second 12-inch skewer. Repeat with remaining shrimp, alternating direction of heads and tails, packing 6 to 8 shrimp tightly onto each pair of skewers.

3. Remove grits from oven and increase oven temperature to 450 degrees. Stir cheddar into grits and season with salt and pepper to taste. Lay shrimp skewers widthwise across baking dish so that shrimp hover over grits. Continue to bake grits and shrimp until shrimp are opaque throughout and grits have thickened slightly, about 10 minutes.

4. Meanwhile, microwave remaining 3 tablespoons melted butter, remaining 1 teaspoon chili powder, chipotle chile powder, and ⅛ teaspoon salt until fragrant, about 20 seconds.

5. Carefully remove dish from oven and transfer shrimp skewers to plate. Stir grits thoroughly, then portion into serving bowls. Remove shrimp from skewers and place on top of grits. Drizzle with spice butter, sprinkle with scallion greens, and serve with lime wedges.

# corned beef hash with poached eggs

*why this recipe works* Corned beef hash is the ultimate comfort food, its warm, runny eggs nestled among salty, seasoned corned beef and tender pieces of potato making for a laid-back, fuss-free brunch. To prepare a homey hash from scratch, we gave starchy russet potatoes a head start by cooking them in boiling water, shortening their skillet cooking time without turning them mushy. Smoky bacon, garlic, and thyme established our hash's aromatic base, and stirring in thick slabs of deli corned beef cut into ¼-inch pieces (rather than the tinny, pasty canned variety) promised rich meaty bites. When we added the potatoes, we encouraged profound browning by packing them down against the bottom of the hot pan. A hit of heavy cream gave the hash some moisture and richness while a touch of hot sauce introduced some welcome heat. We allowed the hash to build up a distinct crust by cooking it undisturbed for a few minutes before flipping it in large portions using a spatula. For runny, just-set eggs, we saved poaching for last, cracking the eggs into individual wells in the hash, covering the pan, and cooking them over low heat. With that, we had a complexly flavored and supremely satisfying corned beef hash. You will need a 12-inch nonstick skillet with a tight-fitting lid for this recipe.

*serves 4*
*total time: 45 minutes*

2 pounds russet potatoes, peeled and cut into ½-inch pieces

Salt and pepper

4 slices bacon, chopped

1 onion, chopped fine

2 garlic cloves, minced

½ teaspoon minced fresh thyme

1 pound corned beef, cut into ¼-inch dice

⅓ cup heavy cream

¼ teaspoon hot sauce

4 large eggs

1. Bring potatoes, 5 cups water, and ½ teaspoon salt to boil in medium saucepan over medium-high heat. Once boiling, cook potatoes for 4 minutes, then drain and set potatoes aside.

2. Cook bacon in 12-inch nonstick skillet over medium-high heat for 2 minutes. Add onion and cook until well browned, about 8 minutes. Add garlic and thyme and cook for 30 seconds. Stir in corned beef. Mix in potatoes and lightly pack mixture with spatula. Reduce heat to medium and pour heavy cream and hot sauce over hash. Cook without stirring for 4 minutes. Flip hash, 1 portion at a time, and fold browned bits back into hash. Lightly repack hash into skillet. Repeat process every minute or two until potatoes are cooked, about 8 minutes longer.

3. Make 4 indentations (about 2 inches wide) in surface of hash using back of spoon. Crack 1 egg into each indentation and season eggs with salt and pepper. Reduce heat to medium-low, cover, and cook until whites are just set and yolks are still runny, 4 to 6 minutes. Cut into 4 wedges, making sure each wedge contains 1 egg, and serve.

# lamb hash with swiss chard, potatoes, and poached eggs

*why this recipe works* This Moroccan-inspired hash is a bold upgrade to your usual brunch fare, boasting spiced lamb, tender potatoes, hearty bites of chard, and a runny egg in every serving. Giving cut-up russet potatoes a jump-start in the microwave kept the recipe efficient. Ground lamb offered a meaty, savory counterpoint to the potatoes, and its rendered fat infused the dish with richness; some aromatics and warm spices like cumin, coriander, and paprika balanced out the deep flavors. Swiss chard lent its bitter, vegetal flavor to the dish, keeping it from tasting overly rich. Because we were combining ingredients that cook at different rates, we prepared each element separately before mixing them together. Once the potatoes, chard, and lamb were all back in the skillet, we pressed the mixture down to ensure good contact with the hot pan, building up deep, delicious browning and a crisp, crunchy exterior on our hash. Flipping the hash in portions was easier than flipping the whole thing at once. Finally, we cooked the eggs right in the hash by making divots with a spoon. You will need a 12-inch nonstick skillet with a tight-fitting lid for this recipe. If the potatoes aren't getting brown in step 4, turn up the heat.

*serves 4*
*total time: 45 minutes*

1½ **pounds russet potatoes, peeled and cut into ½-inch pieces**

2 **tablespoons extra-virgin olive oil**

**Salt and pepper**

1½ **pounds Swiss chard, stems sliced ¼ inch thick, leaves sliced into ½-inch-wide strips**

8 **ounces ground lamb**

1 **onion, chopped fine**

3 **garlic cloves, minced**

2 **teaspoons paprika**

1 **teaspoon ground cumin**

1 **teaspoon ground coriander**

¼ **teaspoon cayenne pepper**

4 **large eggs**

1 **tablespoon minced fresh chives**

1. Toss potatoes with 1 tablespoon oil, ½ teaspoon salt, and ¼ teaspoon pepper in bowl. Cover and microwave until potatoes are translucent around edges, 7 to 9 minutes, stirring halfway through microwaving; drain well.

2. Heat remaining 1 tablespoon oil in 12-inch nonstick skillet over medium-high heat until shimmering. Add chard stems and ¼ teaspoon salt and cook until softened and lightly browned, 5 to 7 minutes. Stir in chard leaves, 1 handful at a time, and cook until mostly wilted, about 4 minutes; transfer to bowl with potatoes.

3. Cook lamb in now-empty skillet over medium-high heat, breaking up meat with wooden spoon, until beginning to brown, about 5 minutes. Stir in onion and cook until softened and lightly browned, 5 to 7 minutes. Stir in garlic, paprika, cumin, coriander, and cayenne and cook until fragrant, about 30 seconds.

4. Stir in chard-potato mixture. Using back of spatula, gently pack chard-potato mixture into skillet and cook, without stirring, for 2 minutes. Flip hash, 1 portion at a time, and lightly repack into skillet. Repeat flipping process every few minutes until potatoes are well browned, 6 to 8 minutes.

5. Make 4 indentations (about 2 inches wide) in surface of hash using back of spoon. Crack 1 egg into each indentation and season eggs with salt and pepper. Reduce heat to medium-low, cover, and cook until whites are just set and yolks are still runny, 4 to 6 minutes. Sprinkle with chives and serve immediately.

# salmon cakes

*why this recipe works* Moist yet crisp with clear fish flavor, these salmon cakes strike the perfect balance between elegant brunch fare and cozy comfort food. Using fresh salmon was essential for cakes with perfectly moist, appealingly chunky texture, and our make-ahead-friendly approach kept things convenient. Chopped in the food processor, bound together with mayo and fresh bread crumbs, and flavored with shallot and Dijon, the assembled cakes stored nicely for later use, and when seared golden brown in a hot skillet and served with a squeeze of lemon, they offered a fresh, sophisticated addition to brunch. Be sure to process the fish in three separate batches and for no more than four pulses, or it will turn to paste. If you don't have a food processor, chop the salmon by hand, freezing it for 10 minutes before chopping. If you find that the bread crumbs are browning too quickly in step 3, reduce the heat. Serve with Avocado-Orange Relish (recipe follows) or Lemon-Dill Sauce (page 72).

*serves 4*
*total time: 30 minutes*
*(plus 1 hour chilling time)*

1½ slices hearty white sandwich bread, torn into 1-inch pieces

1 pound skinless salmon, cut into 1-inch pieces

1 shallot, minced

3 tablespoons mayonnaise

2 tablespoons minced fresh parsley

2 teaspoons Dijon mustard

⅛ teaspoon salt

⅛ teaspoon pepper

1 tablespoon vegetable oil

Lemon wedges

1. Pulse bread in food processor to coarse crumbs, about 4 pulses; transfer to large bowl. Working in 3 batches, pulse salmon in now-empty processor until coarsely chopped into ¼-inch pieces, about 2 pulses, transferring each batch to bowl with bread crumbs. Gently mix until thoroughly combined.

2. Whisk shallot, mayonnaise, parsley, mustard, salt, and pepper together in separate bowl, then gently fold into salmon mixture until just combined. Divide salmon mixture into 4 equal portions and pack into 3-inch-wide cakes. Cover and refrigerate cakes for at least 1 hour.

3. Heat oil in 12-inch nonstick skillet over medium heat until shimmering. Gently lay cakes in skillet and cook until crisp and well browned on first side, 4 to 5 minutes. Gently flip cakes and continue to cook until golden brown on second side and cakes register 125 to 130 degrees, about 4 minutes. Serve with lemon wedges.

## to make ahead

Salmon cakes, prepared through step 2, can be refrigerated for up to 24 hours or frozen for up to 1 month. To cook, continue with step 3, browning cakes for about 3 minutes per side; then, transfer cakes to wire rack set in rimmed baking sheet and bake in 400-degree oven on middle rack until cakes register 125 to 130 degrees, 10 to 12 minutes.

## avocado-orange relish
*makes about 1½ cups*
*For a spicier relish, add some of the jalapeño chile seeds.*

1 large orange, peeled and cut into ½-inch pieces

1 avocado, halved, pitted, and cut into ½-inch pieces

2 tablespoons finely chopped red onion

4 teaspoons lime juice

1 small jalapeño chile, stemmed, seeded, and minced

2 tablespoons minced fresh cilantro

Salt and pepper

Combine all ingredients in bowl, let sit for 15 minutes, and season with salt and pepper to taste. Serve immediately.

# oven-poached salmon with lemon-dill sauce

*why this recipe works* This pair of poached sides of salmon is the perfect brunch centerpiece: It sets a sophisticated tone, serves a crowd, and can be prepared a day or two in advance. We eliminated the need for an oversized pot or a special fish poacher by steaming the fish in its own moisture. We topped two sides of salmon with vinegar, fresh tarragon, and sliced lemons; wrapped them in heavy-duty aluminum foil; and placed them directly on the oven racks in a relatively cool 250-degree oven. Cooked low and slow, the gently steamed salmon emerged perfectly moist and rich. After letting the sides chill for at least an hour, we served this simple but stately salmon with a dollop of cool, creamy lemon-dill sauce for an elegant finish. Be sure to follow our directions for wrapping the salmon in foil; otherwise, the fish's juices may leak onto the bottom of your oven. To test the fish for doneness, simply poke an instant-read thermometer right through the top of the foil. If your sides of salmon are larger, they will have slightly longer cooking times.

*serves 12*
*total time: 1 hour 15 minutes*
*(plus 1 hour 30 minutes cooling and chilling time)*

**salmon**
2 (2½- to 3-pound) skin-on sides of salmon, pinbones removed

Salt

3 tablespoons cider or white wine vinegar

8 sprigs plus 3 tablespoons minced fresh tarragon

3 lemons, sliced thin, plus lemon wedges for serving

**lemon-dill sauce**
2 cups sour cream

2 shallots, minced

2 tablespoons minced fresh dill

1 tablespoon lemon juice

Salt and pepper

**1. for the salmon** Adjust oven racks to upper-middle and lower-middle positions and heat oven to 250 degrees. For each side of salmon, cut 3 sheets heavy-duty aluminum foil about 1 foot longer than fish. Overlap 2 pieces of foil lengthwise by 1 inch and fold to secure seam. Lay third sheet of foil over seam and coat well with vegetable oil spray.

**2.** Lay fish down center of foil, season with salt, sprinkle with vinegar, and arrange tarragon sprigs and lemon slices on top. Fold foil over top of fish and crimp edges of foil together to seal; leave a slight air pocket between top of fish and foil.

**3.** Lay foil-wrapped fish directly on oven racks (without baking sheet) and cook until color of flesh has turned from pink to orange and fish registers 140 degrees, 1 to 1¼ hours. Remove fish from oven, open foil packets, and discard lemon slices and herbs. Let salmon cool on foil at room temperature for 30 minutes.

**4.** Pour off any accumulated liquid, reseal salmon in foil, and refrigerate until cold, at least 1 hour.

**5. for the lemon-dill sauce** Combine all ingredients in serving bowl and season with salt and pepper to taste. Cover and refrigerate until flavors meld, at least 30 minutes.

**6.** Unwrap salmon and brush away any gelled poaching liquid. Carefully transfer fish to serving platters. Sprinkle with minced tarragon and serve with lemon wedges and lemon-dill sauce.

**to make ahead**
Salmon can be refrigerated for up to 2 days in step 4. Let sit at room temperature for 30 minutes before serving. Sauce can be refrigerated for up to 24 hours.

# moroccan chicken salad with apricots and almonds

*why this recipe works* This chicken salad stands out for its crunch and bright, fresh flavors, adding a pop to any brunch spread. With a nod to the warm, summery flavors of Morocco, we paired tender chicken breasts with sweet apricots, zippy lemon, and warm spices. Searing the breasts first imparted some light browning, giving the mild meat a flavor boost, and while it cooled we focused on the chicken's lively accompaniments. To give our dressing nuanced flavor, we reached for garam masala, a traditional spice blend of coriander, cumin, ginger, cinnamon, and black pepper. We also added a little more coriander, honey, and smoked paprika for depth. Blooming the spices in the microwave unlocked their flavors for an even bolder dressing. Convenient canned chickpeas lent heartiness, and crisp romaine combined with slightly bitter watercress made the perfect bed of greens for our toppings. We tossed the salad's lively components together and waited to dress it until serving time, allowing the crisp greens, the crunch of the toasted almonds, the sweetness of the apricots, and the perfectly cooked chicken to all shine (while conveniently keeping the recipe make-ahead friendly).

*serves 4 to 6*
*total time: 1 hour*

**1½ pounds boneless, skinless chicken breasts, trimmed**

**Salt and pepper**

**¾ cup extra-virgin olive oil**

**1 teaspoon garam masala**

**½ teaspoon ground coriander**

**Pinch smoked paprika**

**¼ cup lemon juice (2 lemons)**

**1 tablespoon honey**

**1 (15-ounce) can chickpeas, rinsed**

**¾ cup dried apricots, chopped coarse**

**1 shallot, sliced thin**

**2 tablespoons minced fresh parsley**

**2 romaine lettuce hearts (12 ounces), cut into 1-inch pieces**

**4 ounces (4 cups) watercress**

**½ cup whole almonds, toasted and chopped coarse**

**1.** Pat chicken dry with paper towels and season with salt and pepper. Heat 1 tablespoon oil in 12-inch skillet over medium-high heat until just smoking. Brown chicken well on first side, 6 to 8 minutes. Flip chicken, add ½ cup water, and cover. Reduce heat to medium-low and continue to cook until chicken registers 160 degrees, 5 to 7 minutes. Transfer chicken to cutting board, let cool slightly, then slice ½ inch thick on bias. Let cool to room temperature, about 15 minutes.

**2.** Meanwhile, microwave 1 tablespoon oil, garam masala, coriander, and paprika in medium bowl until oil is hot and fragrant, about 30 seconds. Whisk 3 tablespoons lemon juice, honey, ¼ teaspoon salt, and ¼ teaspoon pepper into spice mixture. Whisking constantly, drizzle in remaining oil.

**3.** In large bowl, combine cooled chicken, chickpeas, apricots, shallot, parsley, and half of dressing and toss to coat. Let mixture sit for 15 to 30 minutes. Whisk remaining 1 tablespoon lemon juice into remaining dressing.

**4.** Toss romaine, watercress, and almonds together in serving bowl, drizzle remaining dressing over top, and toss to combine. Season with salt and pepper to taste. Top with chicken mixture and serve.

**to make ahead**
Dressed chicken mixture and remaining vinaigrette, prepared through step 3, can be refrigerated separately for up to 2 days. To serve, bring chicken mixture and vinaigrette to room temperature, whisk vinaigrette to recombine, and continue with step 4.

# classic cobb salad

*why this recipe works* This is simply the best version of Cobb salad, with crisp vegetables, tangy blue cheese, tender hard-cooked eggs, and perfectly cooked chicken all carefully dressed in a punchy dressing. For plenty of crunch and flavorful contrast, we paired crisp romaine and spicy watercress for our base. Grape tomatoes promised fresh tomato flavor regardless of season, and smooth bites of avocado and hard-cooked egg gave the salad some heft. Broiling was the easiest, most hands-off way to prepare the chicken, delivering nicely browned breasts in minutes. For the vinaigrette, we kept the classic ingredients in play—oil, red wine vinegar, lemon, Worcestershire, and garlic—but also whisked in Dijon for complexity and sugar to balance the piquancy of the savory ingredients. We tossed the ingredients separately in a modest amount of dressing and arranged them over the greens in colorful rows. Sprinkled with blue cheese, chives, and bacon, this salad was a striking, full-flavored beauty. You'll need a large platter or a wide, shallow pasta bowl to accommodate this salad. Though watercress is traditional, feel free to substitute an equal amount of arugula, chicory, curly endive, or a mixture of assertive greens. We prefer grape tomatoes here, but cherry tomatoes can also be used.

*serves 6 to 8*
*total time: 45 minutes*

*vinaigrette*
½ cup extra-virgin olive oil

2 tablespoons red wine vinegar

2 teaspoons lemon juice

1 teaspoon Worcestershire sauce

1 teaspoon Dijon mustard

1 garlic clove, minced

½ teaspoon salt

¼ teaspoon sugar

⅛ teaspoon pepper

*salad*
8 slices bacon, cut into ¼-inch pieces

3 (6-ounce) boneless, skinless chicken breasts, trimmed

Salt and pepper

1 large head romaine lettuce (14 ounces), torn into bite-size pieces

4 ounces (4 cups) watercress, torn into bite-size pieces

10 ounces grape tomatoes, halved

2 avocados, halved, pitted, and cut into ½-inch pieces

3 hard-cooked large eggs, cut into ½-inch pieces

2 ounces blue cheese, crumbled (½ cup)

3 tablespoons minced fresh chives

**1. for the vinaigrette** Whisk all ingredients in medium bowl until well combined; set aside.

**2. for the salad** Cook bacon in 10-inch skillet over medium heat until crispy, 5 to 7 minutes. Using slotted spoon, transfer bacon to paper towel–lined plate and set aside. Season chicken with salt and pepper. Adjust oven rack 6 inches from broiler element and heat broiler. Set broiler pan top in broiler pan bottom and spray with vegetable oil spray.

**3.** Place chicken on prepared broiler pan top and broil until lightly browned, 4 to 8 minutes. Using tongs, flip chicken and broil until chicken registers 160 degrees, 6 to 8 minutes. Transfer to cutting board and let rest for 5 minutes. When cool enough to handle, cut chicken into ½-inch cubes and set aside.

**4.** Combine lettuce and watercress with 5 tablespoons vinaigrette in large bowl and toss to coat; arrange on very large, flat serving platter. Add chicken and ¼ cup vinaigrette to now-empty bowl and toss to coat; arrange in row along 1 edge of greens.

**5.** Add tomatoes and 1 tablespoon vinaigrette to again-empty bowl and toss gently to coat; arrange on opposite edge of greens. Arrange avocados and eggs in separate rows near center of greens and drizzle with remaining vinaigrette. Sprinkle blue cheese, chives, and bacon evenly over salad and serve immediately.

# salade niçoise

*why this recipe works*  Like a Riviera farmer's market's bounty on a single platter, *salade niçoise* is a simple but elegant salad perfectly suited to brunch. A lightly dressed selection of lettuce, green beans, potatoes, hard-cooked eggs, tomatoes, and tuna makes up the bulk of this salad, but it gets its piquant flavor from traditional Mediterranean ingredients like capers, olives, and anchovies. We dressed each element in a caper-herb vinaigrette for a harmonious finished dish, tossing our boiled potatoes in the dressing while still warm so they could sop up plenty of herbal flavor. If you prepare all of the vegetables before cooking the potatoes, this salad comes together easily. Niçoise olives are the classic garnish of salade niçoise. If they're not available, substitute another small, black brined olive; do not use canned. Use small red potatoes measuring 2 inches in diameter. You may need to whisk the dressing to re-emulsify. Leave some space between the arranged mounds so that leaves of lettuce show through.

*serves 4 to 6*
*total time: 45 minutes*

*dressing*

**2 tablespoons white wine vinegar**

**1 teaspoon mayonnaise**

**1 teaspoon Dijon mustard**

**Salt and pepper**

**6 tablespoons extra-virgin olive oil**

**2 tablespoons minced fresh tarragon**

**2 teaspoons minced shallot**

**2 teaspoons chopped capers**

*salad*

**12 ounces red potatoes, unpeeled, quartered**

**Salt and pepper**

**1 head Boston or Bibb lettuce (8 ounces), torn into bite-size pieces**

**2 (5-ounce) cans solid white tuna in water, drained and flaked**

**3 small tomatoes, cored and cut into ½-inch-thick wedges**

**½ small red onion, sliced thin**

**6 ounces green beans, trimmed and halved**

**2 hard-cooked large eggs, peeled and quartered**

**¼ cup pitted niçoise olives**

**6 anchovy fillets, rinsed (optional)**

**1. for the dressing**  Whisk vinegar, mayonnaise, mustard, and ¼ teasoon salt together in small bowl. Whisking constantly, slowly drizzle in oil. Whisk in tarragon, shallot, and capers and season with salt and pepper to taste.

**2. for the salad**  Place potatoes in large saucepan, add water to cover by 1 inch, and bring to boil over high heat. Add 1½ teaspoons salt, reduce to simmer, and cook until potatoes are tender and paring knife can be slipped in and out of potatoes with little resistance, 5 to 8 minutes. With slotted spoon, gently transfer potatoes to bowl (do not discard water). Toss warm potatoes with 2 tablespoons vinaigrette; set aside.

**3.** While potatoes cook, gently toss lettuce with 2 tablespoons vinaigrette in separate bowl until evenly coated. Arrange bed of lettuce on very large flat serving platter. Place tuna in now-empty bowl and break up with fork. Add 2 tablespoons vinaigrette and stir to combine. Mound tuna in center of lettuce. In again-empty bowl, toss tomatoes and onion with 1 tablespoon vinaigrette and season with salt and pepper to taste. Arrange tomato-onion mixture in mound at edge of lettuce bed. Arrange reserved potatoes in separate mound at edge of lettuce bed.

**4.** Return water to boil and add green beans. Cook until crisp-tender, 3 to 5 minutes. Meanwhile, fill large bowl halfway with ice and water. Drain green beans, transfer to ice water, and let sit until just cool, about 30 seconds. Transfer beans to triple layer of paper towels and dry well. In again-empty bowl, toss green beans with remaining vinaigrette. Arrange in separate mound at edge of lettuce bed.

**5.** Arrange eggs, olives, and anchovies, if using, in separate mounds at edge of lettuce bed. Serve.

# shrimp rémoulade

*why this recipe works* Bringing the bold flavors of the Big Easy and offering some tangy contrast to heavy, rich brunch staples, our cool, creamy shrimp rémoulade serves well as a refreshing main or elegant brunch side dish. Rather than calling for a laundry list of ingredients, this shrimp salad captures rémoulade's distinct flavor thanks to a few easy-to-source items. We worked with eye-catching jumbo shrimp, gently poaching them in salty water for a tender texture and full, even seasoning. We prepared our own signature rémoulade sauce using pantry items, starting with mayonnaise as the base. Spicy brown mustard proved a strong stand-in for hard-to-find Creole mustard's distinct heat, especially once we boosted it with horseradish and a touch of cayenne. Crunchy cornichons delivered bite and texture, scallions and lemon juice added a fresh pop, and ketchup and paprika delivered extra complexity and appealing color. Stirring the shrimp into this simple rémoulade and chilling it for an hour allowed the flavors to meld before we proudly plated our tender, saucy shrimp on buttery leaves of Bibb lettuce. We prefer shrimp not treated with sodium or preservatives such as sodium tripolyphosphate (STPP). Most frozen E-Z peel shrimp have been treated (the ingredient list should tell you). If using treated shrimp, reduce the salt in step 1 to ½ teaspoon.

*serves 4*
*total time: 30 minutes*
*(plus 1 hour chilling time)*

*shrimp*
1½ pounds jumbo shrimp (16 to 20 per pound), peeled, deveined, and tails removed

Salt and pepper

*rémoulade*
⅔ cup mayonnaise

¼ cup finely chopped celery

¼ cup finely chopped green bell pepper

3 tablespoons minced cornichons

2 scallions, sliced thin

1 tablespoon lemon juice

1½ teaspoons prepared horseradish, drained

1 teaspoon spicy brown mustard

1 teaspoon ketchup

1 garlic clove, minced

½ teaspoon paprika

½ teaspoon Worcestershire sauce

¼ teaspoon salt

¼ teaspoon pepper

⅛ teaspoon cayenne pepper

½ head Bibb lettuce (4 ounces), leaves separated and torn

Lemon wedges

Hot sauce

**1. for the shrimp** Combine 3 cups water, shrimp, and 1½ teaspoons salt in Dutch oven. Set pot over medium-high heat and cook, stirring occasionally, until water registers 170 degrees and shrimp are just beginning to turn pink, 5 to 7 minutes.

**2.** Remove pot from heat, cover, and let sit until shrimp are completely pink and firm, about 5 minutes. Drain shrimp in colander. Rinse shrimp under cold water, then pat dry with paper towels. Transfer shrimp to large bowl and refrigerate until ready to use.

**3. for the rémoulade** Combine all ingredients in bowl.

**4.** Fold rémoulade into shrimp until combined. Season with salt and pepper to taste. Cover and refrigerate to let flavors blend, about 1 hour. Serve over lettuce with lemon wedges and hot sauce.

quiches, tarts,
and casseroles

# leek and goat cheese quiche

*why this recipe works* This quiche's velvety custard makes it perfect for an elegant affair or a laid-back brunch. Store-bought pie dough, partially baked and still warm, can be used in place of the homemade crust.

*serves 6 to 8*
*total time: 3 hours 30 minutes*
*(plus 2 hours 45 minutes chilling and cooling time)*

## crust
**3 tablespoons ice water, plus extra as needed**

**4 teaspoons sour cream**

**1¼ cups (6¼ ounces) all-purpose flour**

**1½ teaspoons sugar**

**½ teaspoon salt**

**8 tablespoons unsalted butter, cut into ¼-inch pieces and frozen for 10 to 15 minutes**

## filling
**2 tablespoons unsalted butter**

**1 pound leeks, white and green parts only, chopped fine**

**¾ teaspoon salt**

**5 large eggs**

**2 cups half-and-half**

**¼ teaspoon pepper**

**4 ounces goat cheese, crumbled (1 cup)**

**1 tablespoon minced fresh chives**

**1. for the crust** Whisk ice water and sour cream together in bowl. Process flour, sugar, and salt in food processor until combined, about 3 seconds. Scatter frozen butter over top and pulse mixture until butter is size of large peas, about 10 pulses.

**2.** Pour half of sour cream mixture over flour mixture and pulse until incorporated, about 3 pulses. Repeat with remaining sour cream

mixture. Pinch dough with your fingers; if dough feels dry and does not hold together, sprinkle 1 to 2 tablespoons more ice water over mixture and pulse until dough forms large clumps and no dry flour remains, 3 to 5 pulses.

**3.** Turn dough onto sheet of plastic wrap and flatten into 4-inch disk. Wrap tightly and refrigerate for at least 1 hour or up to 2 days. Before rolling dough out, let it sit on counter to soften slightly, about 10 minutes.

**4.** Roll dough between 2 large sheets parchment paper to 12-inch circle. (If dough is soft or sticky, refrigerate until firm.) Remove parchment on top of dough round and flip into 9-inch pie plate; peel off second sheet of parchment. Lift dough and press into pie plate. Cover loosely with plastic and refrigerate until firm, about 30 minutes.

**5.** Trim all but ½ inch of dough overhanging edge of pie plate. Tuck dough underneath to form tidy, even edge that sits on lip of pie plate. Crimp dough evenly around edge of pie plate using your fingers. Wrap dough-lined pie plate loosely in plastic and refrigerate until firm, about 15 minutes.

**6.** Adjust oven rack to middle position and heat oven to 400 degrees. Line chilled crust with double layer of aluminum foil, covering edges to prevent burning, and fill with pie weights or pennies. Bake until dough looks dry and is pale in color,

25 to 30 minutes. Transfer to rimmed baking sheet and remove weights and foil.

**7. for the filling** Reduce oven to 350 degrees. Melt butter in 10-inch nonstick skillet over medium-high heat. Add leeks and ½ teaspoon salt and cook until softened, about 6 minutes; transfer to bowl.

**8.** Whisk eggs, half-and-half, ¼ teaspoon salt, and pepper together in large bowl. Stir in leeks and goat cheese. Place pie shell in oven and carefully pour egg mixture into warm shell until it reaches ½ inch from top of crust (you may have extra egg mixture).

**9.** Bake quiche until top is lightly browned, center is set but soft, and knife inserted about 1 inch from edge comes out clean, 40 to 50 minutes. Let quiche cool for at least 1 hour or up to 3 hours. Sprinkle with chives. Serve slightly warm or at room temperature.

### variation
**spinach and feta quiche**
Omit chives and substitute crumbled feta for goat cheese. Stir 1 (10-ounce) package frozen chopped spinach, thawed and squeezed dry, into eggs with cheese.

### to make ahead
Cooled quiche can be refrigerated wrapped in plastic wrap for up to 6 hours. Reheat in 350-degree oven for 10 to 15 minutes.

# french onion and bacon tart

*why this recipe works* This bistro classic is as refined as it is rich. We kept the filling onion-forward by cooking the strands in rendered bacon fat and stirring them into a light custard. Use yellow or white onions here; sweet onions will make the tart too sweet. Use a 9-inch tinned-steel tart pan.

*serves 6 to 8*
*total time: 1 hour 15 minutes*
*(plus 30 minutes chilling time)*

*crust*
1¼ cups (6¼ ounces) all-purpose flour

1 tablespoon sugar

½ teaspoon salt

8 tablespoons unsalted butter, cut into ½-inch cubes and chilled

2–3 tablespoons ice water

*filling*
4 slices bacon, cut into ¼-inch pieces

Vegetable oil

1½ pounds onions, halved through root end and cut crosswise into ¼-inch slices

¾ teaspoon salt

1 sprig fresh thyme

2 large eggs

½ cup half-and-half

¼ teaspoon pepper

**1. for the crust** Spray 9-inch tart pan with removable bottom with vegetable oil spray. Pulse flour, sugar, and salt in food processor until combined, about 4 pulses. Scatter butter over top and pulse until mixture resembles coarse sand, about 15 pulses. Add 2 tablespoons ice water and process until clumps form and no powdery bits remain, about 5 seconds, adding up to 1 tablespoon more ice water if dough will not form clumps.

**2.** Tear dough into walnut-size pieces and sprinkle evenly in pan. Working outward from center, press dough into even layer, sealing any cracks. Working around edge, press dough firmly into corners, up sides of pan, and into fluted ridges. Use your thumb to level off top edge of dough. Use excess dough to patch any holes. Lay plastic wrap over dough and smooth out any bumps or shallow areas. Place dough-lined pan on plate and freeze for 30 minutes.

**3.** Adjust oven rack to middle position and heat oven to 375 degrees. Place frozen tart shell on baking sheet. Spray piece of extra-wide heavy-duty aluminum foil with vegetable oil spray and gently press against dough, covering edges to prevent burning. Fill with pie weights and bake until top edge of dough just starts to color and surface no longer looks wet, about 30 minutes. Remove foil and weights. Return sheet to oven and continue to bake until tart shell is golden brown, 5 to 10 minutes longer. Set sheet with tart shell on wire rack. Do not turn off oven.

**4. for the filling** Meanwhile, cook bacon in 12-inch nonstick skillet over medium heat until crispy, 5 to 7 minutes. Using slotted spoon, transfer bacon to paper towel–lined plate. Pour off all but 2 tablespoons fat from skillet (if you do not have 2 tablespoons fat, add vegetable oil as needed to make this amount).

**5.** Add onions, salt, and thyme sprig to skillet. Cover and cook until onions release liquid and start to wilt, about 10 minutes. Reduce heat to low and continue to cook, covered, until onions are very soft, about 20 minutes longer, stirring once or twice (if after 15 minutes onions look wet, uncover and continue to cook 5 minutes longer). Remove pan from heat and let onions cool for 5 minutes.

**6.** Whisk eggs, half-and-half, and pepper together in large bowl. Discard thyme sprig. Stir onions into egg mixture until just incorporated. Spread onion mixture over tart shell and sprinkle bacon evenly over top. Bake tart on sheet until center feels firm to touch, 20 to 25 minutes, rotating pan halfway through baking.

**7.** Transfer sheet to wire rack and let tart cool for at least 10 minutes. Remove outer metal ring of tart pan, slide thin metal spatula between tart and pan bottom, and carefully slide tart onto platter. Serve warm or at room temperature.

**to make ahead**
Cooled tart can be refrigerated wrapped in plastic wrap for up to 3 days. Reheat on baking sheet in 325-degree oven for 10 to 15 minutes.

# spanakopita

*why this recipe works* Our brunch-ready spanakopita boasts the flakiest crust possible because it is baked in a broad, shallow baking sheet, maximizing the phyllo's exposure to the oven's dry heat. We wilted spinach in the microwave, squeezing out its moisture before stirring in tangy crumbled feta, rich Greek yogurt, and aromatic Pecorino Romano. If you can't find curly-leaf spinach, substitute flat-leaf spinach; do not use baby spinach. Full-fat sour cream can be substituted for the Greek yogurt. Phyllo is also available in 18 by 14-inch sheets; if using, cut them in half to make 14 by 9-inch sheets. Do not thaw the phyllo in the microwave; let it sit in the refrigerator overnight or on the counter for 4 to 5 hours.

*serves 6 to 8*
*total time: 1 hour*

*filling*
20 ounces curly-leaf spinach, stemmed

¼ cup water

12 ounces feta cheese, rinsed, patted dry, and crumbled into fine pieces (about 3 cups)

¾ cup whole-milk Greek yogurt

4 scallions, sliced thin

2 large eggs, lightly beaten

¼ cup minced fresh mint

2 tablespoons minced fresh dill

3 garlic cloves, minced

1 teaspoon grated lemon zest plus 1 tablespoon juice

1 teaspoon ground nutmeg

½ teaspoon pepper

¼ teaspoon salt

⅛ teaspoon cayenne pepper

*phyllo layers*
7 tablespoons unsalted butter, melted

8 ounces (14 by 9-inch) phyllo, thawed

1½ ounces Pecorino Romano cheese, grated (¾ cup)

2 teaspoons sesame seeds (optional)

**1. for the filling** Place spinach and water in bowl. Cover and microwave until spinach is wilted and volume is halved, about 5 minutes. Remove bowl from microwave and keep covered for 1 minute. Transfer spinach to colander and gently press to release liquid. Transfer spinach to cutting board and chop coarse. Return to colander and press again. Stir spinach and remaining ingredients in bowl until thoroughly combined.

**2. for the phyllo layers** Adjust oven rack to lower-middle position and heat oven to 425 degrees. Line rimmed baking sheet with parchment paper. Using pastry brush, lightly brush 14 by 9-inch rectangle in center of parchment with melted butter to cover area same size as phyllo. Lay 1 phyllo sheet on buttered parchment and brush thoroughly with melted butter. Repeat with 9 more phyllo sheets, brushing each with melted butter (you should have total of 10 layers of phyllo).

**3.** Spread spinach mixture evenly on phyllo, leaving ¼-inch border on all sides. Cover spinach with 6 more phyllo sheets, brushing each with butter and sprinkling each with about 2 tablespoons Pecorino. Lay 2 more phyllo sheets on top, brushing each with melted butter (these layers should not be sprinkled with Pecorino).

**4.** Working from center outward, use palms of your hands to compress layers and press out any air pockets. Using sharp knife, score spanakopita through top 3 layers of phyllo into 24 equal pieces. Sprinkle with sesame seeds, if using. Bake until phyllo is golden and crisp, 20 to 25 minutes. Let spanakopita cool on sheet for at least 10 minutes or up to 2 hours. Slide spanakopita, still on parchment, to cutting board. Cut into squares and serve.

**to make ahead**
Filling can be made and refrigerated up to 24 hours in advance. Assembled spanakopita can be frozen wrapped in plastic wrap for up to 1 month. To make from frozen, increase baking time by 5 to 10 minutes.

# "impossible" ham-and-cheese pie

*why this recipe works* This brunch pie is so named because its "crust" materializes while it bakes, encasing the rich, indulgent filling in a crisp, buttery shell as if by magic. Falling somewhere between a quiche and a strata, "impossible" pies were popular in the 1970s, calling on Bisquick and a handful of stir-ins to turn out an ultraconvenient brunch; our revamped version still keeps things simple while also bringing in fresh, bold flavors. For a savory filling that baked up crisp on the outside, forming the "crust," and stayed creamy and custardy, not cakey, on the inside, we prepared a simple but rich mixture of flour, baking powder, half-and-half, and eggs, adding Dijon mustard and nutmeg for some extra nuance. Coating the pie dish with nutty Parmesan cheese ensured flavorful browned edges. We poured the batter over a selection of full-flavored ingredients that minimized prep work—scallions, diced deli ham, and shredded Gruyère—and baked the pie on the lowest rack for maximum exposure to the oven's heat. From its crisp crust-like edges to rich, full-flavored filling, the only thing impossible about this pie was resisting a second slice.

*serves 8*
*total time: 1 hour*

1 tablespoon unsalted butter, softened, plus 2 tablespoons melted

3 tablespoons finely grated Parmesan cheese

8 ounces Gruyère cheese, shredded (2 cups)

4 ounces thickly sliced deli ham, chopped

4 scallions, minced

½ cup (2½ ounces) all-purpose flour

¾ teaspoon baking powder

½ teaspoon pepper

¼ teaspoon salt

1 cup half-and-half

4 large eggs, lightly beaten

2 teaspoons Dijon mustard

⅛ teaspoon ground nutmeg

**1.** Adjust oven rack to lowest position and heat oven to 350 degrees. Grease 9-inch pie plate with softened butter, then coat plate evenly with Parmesan.

**2.** Combine Gruyère, ham, and scallions in bowl. Sprinkle cheese-ham mixture evenly in bottom of prepared plate. Combine flour, baking powder, pepper, and salt in now-empty bowl.

**3.** Whisk half-and-half, eggs, mustard, nutmeg, and melted butter into flour mixture until smooth. Slowly pour batter over cheese-ham mixture in plate.

**4.** Bake until pie is light golden brown and filling is set, 30 to 35 minutes. Let pie cool on wire rack for 15 minutes; slice into wedges and serve warm.

# 24-hour "omelet"

*why this recipe works* Despite its name, this "omelet" is nothing like the filling-stuffed egg dish you expect at brunch, nor does it take a day to bake. This cheesy, golden, puffed casserole is all about the eggs, consisting of a rich custard, bread, and cheese and yielding a melt-in-your-mouth texture that rivals even the fluffiest scrambled eggs. The eggs should be this dish's focus, not the bread, so to keep their flavor at the fore, we prepared a milk-based custard. Buttered white bread, cut into bite-size pieces and layered with tangy cheddar cheese in a baking dish, promised to melt right into the custard while also bringing in plenty of richness. A small amount of grated onion and a bit of dry mustard and hot sauce added just enough complexity to the creamy eggs. Refrigerating the assembled omelet overnight melded the flavors and saturated the bread, so all we had to do before brunch was bake it. Cheesy and golden, this humble casserole puffed impressively above the rim of the baking dish, making it a tempting but unfussy centerpiece. Use the large holes of a box grater to grate the onion. The omelet needs to sit in the refrigerator, well covered, for at least 8 hours in order to achieve the desired consistency.

*serves 6 to 8*
*total time: 1 hour 30 minutes*
*(plus 8 hours chilling time)*

3 tablespoons unsalted butter, softened

10 slices hearty white sandwich bread

12 ounces cheddar cheese, shredded (3 cups)

8 large eggs

3 cups whole milk

1 small onion, grated

1 teaspoon salt

½ teaspoon pepper

1 teaspoon dry mustard

½ teaspoon hot sauce

1. Grease 13 by 9-inch baking dish. Spread butter evenly over 1 side of bread slices, then cut into 1-inch pieces. Scatter half of bread evenly in prepared dish and sprinkle with half of cheddar. Repeat with remaining bread and cheese.

2. Whisk eggs, milk, onion, salt, pepper, mustard, and hot sauce together in bowl until well combined. Pour egg mixture evenly over bread and press lightly on bread to submerge. Wrap dish tightly with plastic wrap and refrigerate for at least 8 hours.

3. Adjust oven rack to middle position and heat oven to 350 degrees. Unwrap casserole and bake until puffed and golden, about 1 hour. Serve immediately.

## variations

**24-hour "omelet" with sun-dried tomatoes and mozzarella**
Substitute mozzarella cheese for cheddar. Add ½ cup grated Parmesan cheese and ½ cup oil-packed sun-dried tomatoes, patted dry and chopped, between 2 layers of bread in step 1. Sprinkle 3 tablespoons minced fresh cilantro over top before serving.

**24-hour "omelet" with pepper jack and chipotle chile**
Substitute pepper Jack cheese for cheddar and 2 to 3 teaspoons minced canned chipotle chile in adobo sauce for dry mustard and hot sauce. Sprinkle 3 tablespoons minced fresh cilantro over top before serving.

### to make ahead
Omelet, prepared through step 2, can be refrigerated for up to 24 hours.

# savory bread pudding with turkey sausage and kale

*why this recipe works* This bread pudding is earthy, comforting, and perfect for a relaxed brunch at home. To make sure this casserole came out rich and satisfying but not overbearing, we chose leaner (but still flavorful) turkey sausage instead of pork and banned soggy bread by toasting torn baguette slices, enriching their flavor and ensuring they would stand up to the custard. To add even more depth to the pudding while further preventing a wet texture, we microwaved kale with some aromatics and oil to jump-start its cooking and eliminate excess water in our finished dish. We stirred the toasted bread into a simple custard, prepared with 3 parts cream to 2 parts milk for measured richness. To prevent curdling, we stabilized the custard by using just yolks rather than the traditional whole eggs. Once the bread had absorbed some of the custard and the kale was mixed in, we layered the custard-bread mixture with sausage and topped it all off with Parmesan. From there, all we had to do was bake it, covered at first to set the filling and then uncovered for the last 20 minutes to generate some appealing browning.

*serves 4 to 6*
*total time: 2 hours*

1 (18- to 20-inch) baguette, torn into 1-inch pieces (10 cups)

1 pound kale, stemmed and chopped

4 shallots, sliced thin

2 garlic cloves, minced

1 teaspoon extra-virgin olive oil

3 cups heavy cream

2 cups whole milk

8 large egg yolks

1 tablespoon Dijon mustard

1 pound turkey sausage, casings removed

¼ cup grated Parmesan cheese

2 tablespoons minced fresh chives

1. Adjust oven rack to middle position and heat oven to 450 degrees. Arrange bread in even layer in 13 by 9-inch baking dish. Bake, stirring occasionally, until bread is crisp and browned, about 12 minutes; let cool for 10 minutes. Reduce oven temperature to 400 degrees.

2. Meanwhile, combine kale, shallots, garlic, and oil in bowl and microwave, stirring occasionally, until kale is wilted, about 5 minutes. Wrap kale mixture in clean dish towel and wring tightly to squeeze out as much liquid as possible.

3. Whisk cream, milk, egg yolks, and mustard together in large bowl. Stir in toasted bread and drained kale mixture until well combined.

4. Spray now-empty baking dish with vegetable oil spray. Pour half of bread mixture into prepared dish. Crumble half of sausage into ½-inch pieces over top. Top with remaining bread mixture and remaining sausage. Sprinkle with Parmesan.

5. Cover tightly with greased aluminum foil and bake for 45 minutes. Uncover and continue to bake until custard is just set and top is browned, about 20 minutes.

6. Remove dish from oven and let cool for 10 minutes. Sprinkle with chives before serving.

# french toast casserole

*why this recipe works* This tempting casserole takes traditional French toast to new heights, delivering sweet, crisp-yet-custardy bread in rich layers meant to satisfy a crowd, no batches necessary. To tie soft yet sturdy bread together with a rich custard, we had to look beyond the ingredients we used in our standard recipe (page 48). Though challah is perfect for stovetop versions, here we found that only the dense texture and thin, chewy crusts of French and Italian loaves could stand up to a moist, heavy custard. We added extra textural insurance by "staling" the bread in the oven, allowing it to dry and toast slightly before assembling the dish. For the custard, we settled on eight whole eggs and a little less than twice as much whole milk as heavy cream, which gave us a rich and custardy but not cloying result. (This is brunch, after all, not dessert.) The assembled casserole needed an extended stay in the fridge for the flavors to meld and the bread to soak up the rich custard. All we had left to do before baking was sprinkle on a sweet, crunchy pecan topping. Rich, just sweet enough, and make-ahead friendly—what more could you ask for? Do not substitute low-fat or skim milk in this recipe. Be sure to use supermarket-style loaf bread with a thin crust and fluffy crumb; artisan loaves with a thick crust and a chewy crumb do not work well here.

*serves 6 to 8*
*total time: 2 hours*
*(plus 8 hours chilling time)*

1 pound French or Italian bread, torn into 1-inch pieces

8 tablespoons unsalted butter, softened, plus extra for baking dish

8 large eggs

2½ cups whole milk

1½ cups heavy cream

1 tablespoon granulated sugar

2 teaspoons vanilla extract

½ teaspoon ground cinnamon

½ teaspoon ground nutmeg

1⅓ cups packed (9⅓ ounces) light brown sugar

3 tablespoons light corn syrup

2 cups pecans, chopped coarse

**1.** Adjust oven racks to upper-middle and lower-middle positions and heat oven to 325 degrees. Spread bread out over 2 rimmed baking sheets and bake until dry and light golden, about 25 minutes, switching and rotating sheets halfway through baking. Let bread cool completely.

**2.** Butter 13 by 9-inch baking dish, then pack dried bread into dish. Whisk eggs, milk, cream, granulated sugar, vanilla, cinnamon, and nutmeg together in bowl. Pour egg mixture evenly over bread and press on bread lightly to submerge. Wrap dish tightly with plastic wrap and refrigerate for at least 8 hours.

**3.** Stir butter, brown sugar, and corn syrup together in bowl until smooth, then stir in pecans.

**4.** Adjust oven rack to middle position and heat oven to 350 degrees. Unwrap casserole and sprinkle evenly with topping, breaking apart any large clumps. Place casserole on rimmed baking sheet and bake until puffed and golden, about 1 hour. Let casserole cool for 10 minutes before serving.

**variation**

rum-raisin french toast casserole
While bread dries, microwave 1½ cups raisins and 1 cup rum in covered bowl until boiling, 1 to 2 minutes. Let sit, covered, until raisins are plump, about 15 minutes. Drain raisins thoroughly, discarding excess rum. Sprinkle raisins between bread pieces when assembling casserole in step 2.

**to make ahead**
Assembled casserole and topping, prepared through step 3, can be refrigerated separately for up to 24 hours.

# new orleans bourbon bread pudding

*why this recipe works* This bread pudding is the perfect sweet, boozy counterpoint to all savory brunch standbys. To keep this pudding rustic but rich, we tore a crusty baguette into pieces and toasted them to keep the bread from turning soggy. We introduced bourbon's rich flavor by simmering raisins in it and later stirring the concentrated liquor into the custard. We layered the spiked custard–soaked bread and raisins into a baking dish, baked it until the custard had a chance to set up, then sprinkled on cinnamon, sugar, and butter for a caramelized finish. For a little more punch, drizzle Bourbon Sauce (recipe follows) over individual servings.

*serves 8 to 10*
*total time: 1 hour 30 minutes*
*(plus 1 hour soaking and*
*cooling time)*

1 (18- to 20-inch) baguette, torn into 1-inch pieces (10 cups)

1 cup golden raisins

¾ cup bourbon

6 tablespoons unsalted butter, cut into 6 pieces and chilled, plus extra for baking dish

8 large egg yolks

1½ cups packed (10½ ounces) light brown sugar

3 cups heavy cream

1 cup whole milk

1 tablespoon vanilla extract

1½ teaspoons ground cinnamon

¼ teaspoon ground nutmeg

¼ teaspoon salt

3 tablespoons granulated sugar

1. Adjust oven rack to middle position and heat oven to 450 degrees. Arrange bread in single layer on baking sheet and bake until crisp and browned, about 12 minutes, turning pieces over and rotating sheet halfway through baking. Let bread cool. Reduce oven temperature to 300 degrees.

2. Meanwhile, heat raisins with ½ cup bourbon in small saucepan over medium-high heat until

bourbon begins to simmer, 2 to 3 minutes. Strain mixture, reserving bourbon and raisins separately.

3. Butter 13 by 9-inch broiler-safe baking dish. Whisk egg yolks, brown sugar, cream, milk, vanilla, 1 teaspoon cinnamon, nutmeg, and salt together in large bowl. Whisk in reserved bourbon plus remaining ¼ cup bourbon. Add toasted bread and toss until evenly coated. Let mixture sit until bread begins to absorb custard, about 30 minutes, tossing occasionally. If majority of bread is still hard, continue to soak for 15 to 20 minutes.

4. Pour half of bread mixture into prepared baking dish and sprinkle with half of raisins. Pour remaining bread mixture into dish and sprinkle with remaining raisins. Cover with aluminum foil and bake for 45 minutes.

5. Meanwhile, mix granulated sugar and remaining ½ teaspoon cinnamon in small bowl. Using your fingers, cut 6 tablespoons butter into sugar mixture until size of small peas. Remove foil from pudding, sprinkle with butter mixture, and bake, uncovered, until custard is just set, 20 to 25 minutes. Remove pudding from oven and heat broiler.

6. Once broiler is heated, broil pudding until top forms golden crust, about 2 minutes. Transfer to wire rack and let cool for at least 30 minutes or up to 2 hours. Serve.

## bourbon sauce
*makes about 1 cup*

¼ cup bourbon

1½ teaspoons cornstarch

¾ cup heavy cream

2 tablespoons sugar

2 teaspoons unsalted butter, cut into small pieces

Pinch salt

Whisk 2 tablespoons bourbon and cornstarch in small bowl until well combined. Heat cream and sugar in small saucepan over medium heat until sugar dissolves. Whisk in cornstarch mixture and bring to boil. Reduce heat to low and cook until sauce thickens, 3 to 5 minutes. Off heat, stir in butter, salt, and remaining 2 tablespoons bourbon. Drizzle warm sauce over individual servings of bread pudding

**to make ahead**
Bourbon Sauce can be refrigerated for up to 5 days; reheat on stovetop.

muffins,
breads,
and
more

# blueberry swirl muffins

*why this recipe works* A great brunch demands great blueberry muffins, and by swirling an intense stovetop jam into each cup along with fresh berries for their juicy bursts, this recipe delivers maximum blueberry flavor. A lemon-scented sugar sprinkled on before baking gives the muffins a sweet, fragrant crust. For finely grated lemon zest, use a rasp grater.

*makes 12 muffins*
*total time: 1 hour*

*lemon-sugar topping*
⅓ cup (2⅓ ounces) **sugar**

1½ teaspoons **grated lemon zest**

*muffins*
10 ounces (2 cups) **blueberries**

1⅛ cups (7¾ ounces) **plus 1 teaspoon sugar**

2½ cups (12½ ounces) **all-purpose flour**

2½ teaspoons **baking powder**

1 teaspoon **salt**

2 large **eggs**

4 tablespoons **unsalted butter, melted and cooled**

¼ cup **vegetable oil**

1 cup **buttermilk**

1½ teaspoons **vanilla extract**

**1. for the lemon-sugar topping** Combine sugar and lemon zest in small bowl and set aside.

**2. for the muffins** Adjust oven rack to upper-middle position and heat oven to 425 degrees. Spray 12-cup muffin tin with vegetable oil spray. Bring 1 cup blueberries and 1 teaspoon sugar to simmer in small saucepan over medium heat. Cook, mashing berries with spoon several times and stirring frequently, until berries have broken down and mixture is thickened and reduced to ¼ cup,

about 6 minutes. Transfer to small bowl and let cool completely, 10 to 15 minutes.

**3.** Whisk flour, baking powder, and salt together in large bowl. Whisk remaining 1⅛ cups sugar and eggs together in medium bowl until thick and homogeneous, about 45 seconds. Slowly whisk in melted butter and oil until combined. Whisk in buttermilk and vanilla until combined. Using rubber spatula, fold egg mixture and remaining 1 cup blueberries into flour mixture until just moistened. (Batter will be very lumpy with few spots of dry flour; do not overmix.)

**4.** Divide batter evenly among prepared muffin cups (batter should completely fill cups and mound slightly). Spoon 1 teaspoon of cooked berry mixture into center of each mound of batter. Using chopstick or skewer, gently swirl berry filling into batter using figure-8 motion. Sprinkle lemon-sugar topping evenly over muffins.

**5.** Bake until muffins are golden brown and toothpick inserted in center comes out with few crumbs attached, 17 to 19 minutes, rotating muffin tin halfway through baking. Let muffins cool in muffin tin for 5 minutes, then transfer to wire rack and let cool for 5 minutes before serving.

## variations

### blueberry swirl muffins with frozen blueberries
Substitute 1⅔ cups frozen blueberries for fresh blueberries. Cook 1 cup blueberries as directed in step 2. Rinse remaining berries under cold running water and dry well. Proceed with recipe as directed.

### blueberry swirl muffins with streusel topping
Omit lemon-sugar topping. Combine ½ cup plus 3 tablespoons all-purpose flour, 3 tablespoons granulated sugar, 3 tablespoons packed dark brown sugar, and pinch salt in small bowl. Drizzle with 5 tablespoons warm, melted unsalted butter and toss with fork until evenly moistened and mixture forms large chunks with some pea-size pieces throughout. Sprinkle streusel topping over muffins before baking.

### blueberry swirl muffins with almond crunch topping
*Turbinado sugar is often sold as Sugar in the Raw.*

Omit lemon-sugar topping. Add ⅓ cup finely ground almonds to flour mixture. Add 1 teaspoon almond extract to batter with vanilla extract. Combine ⅓ cup finely ground almonds and 4 teaspoons turbinado sugar in bowl and sprinkle over muffins before baking.

# savory corn muffins

*why this recipe works* Where many a corn muffin recipe bakes up dry or gritty, ours delivers a bright batch of moist, corn-forward muffins that are simple to prepare and perfect for pairing with any savory brunch main. A 2:1 ratio of cornmeal to flour yielded the strongest corn flavor. Cutting back on sugar kept the flavor savory, but also made for a drier crumb. We made up for this by microwaving some of the cornmeal with milk. The thick, polenta-like porridge allowed us to introduce extra moisture to the batter without thinning it out, ensuring that our muffins still baked up tall and proud. In addition to the milk, we also called on butter and sour cream for richness and added moisture. Don't use coarse-ground or white cornmeal.

*makes 12 muffins*
*total time: 45 minutes*

2 cups (10 ounces) cornmeal

1 cup (5 ounces)
all-purpose flour

1½ teaspoons baking powder

1 teaspoon baking soda

1¼ teaspoons salt

1¼ cups whole milk

1 cup sour cream

8 tablespoons unsalted butter, melted and cooled slightly

3 tablespoons sugar

2 large eggs, beaten

1. Adjust oven rack to upper-middle position and heat oven to 425 degrees. Spray 12-cup muffin tin with vegetable oil spray. Whisk 1½ cups cornmeal, flour, baking powder, baking soda, and salt together in medium bowl.

2. Combine milk and remaining ½ cup cornmeal in large bowl. Microwave milk-cornmeal mixture for 1½ minutes. Whisk thoroughly and continue to microwave, whisking every 30 seconds, until thickened to batter-like consistency (whisk will leave channel in bottom of bowl that slowly fills in), 1 to 3 minutes longer. Whisk in sour cream, melted butter, and sugar until combined. Whisk in eggs until combined. Fold in flour mixture until thoroughly combined.

3. Divide batter evenly among prepared muffin cups (about ½ cup batter per cup; batter will mound slightly above rim). Bake until tops are golden brown and toothpick inserted in center comes out clean, 13 to 17 minutes, rotating muffin tin halfway through baking. Let muffins cool in muffin tin on wire rack for 5 minutes. Remove muffins from muffin tin and let cool 5 minutes longer. Serve warm.

## variations

### savory corn muffins with cheddar and scallions

Add ½ teaspoon pepper, ¼ teaspoon dry mustard, and pinch cayenne to dry ingredients in step 1. Whisk in 1½ cups shredded cheddar cheese and 5 thinly sliced scallions with eggs.

### savory corn muffins with rosemary and black pepper

Whisk in 1 tablespoon minced fresh rosemary and 1½ teaspoons pepper with eggs.

# mixed berry scones

*why this recipe works* These scones are a flaky, honey-glazed brunch delight, brimming with juicy, sweet berries in a buttery, rich crumb. We achieved a perfectly crumbly texture by incorporating butter in two ways, processing some with flour, sugar, baking powder, and salt for even distribution, then pulsing more into pea-size pieces to achieve rich buttery pockets. Tossing frozen berries in confectioners' sugar before folding them into the flour mixture prevented them from bleeding into the dough, and a honey-butter glaze, brushed on partway through baking, gave the scones a sweet sheen. Work the dough as little as possible, just until it comes together. Work quickly to keep the butter and berries as cold as possible for the best results. Note that the butter is divided in this recipe. An equal amount of frozen blueberries, raspberries, blackberries, or strawberries (halved) can be used in place of the mixed berries.

*makes 8 scones*
*total time: 1 hour*

*scones*
**8¾ ounces (1¾ cups) frozen mixed berries**

**3 tablespoons confectioners' sugar**

**3 cups (15 ounces) all-purpose flour**

**12 tablespoons unsalted butter, cut into ½-inch pieces, chilled**

**⅓ cup (2⅓ ounces) granulated sugar**

**1 tablespoon baking powder**

**1¼ teaspoons salt**

**¾ cup plus 2 tablespoons whole milk**

**1 large egg plus 1 large yolk**

*glaze*
**2 tablespoons unsalted butter, melted**

**1 tablespoon honey**

**1. for the scones** Adjust oven rack to upper-middle position and heat oven to 425 degrees. Line rimmed baking sheet with parchment paper. If your berry mix contains strawberries, cut them in half.

Toss berries with confectioners' sugar in bowl; freeze until needed.

**2.** Combine flour, 6 tablespoons butter, granulated sugar, baking powder, and salt in food processor and process until butter is fully incorporated, about 15 seconds. Add remaining 6 tablespoons butter and pulse until butter is reduced to pea-size pieces, 10 to 12 pulses. Transfer mixture to large bowl. Stir in berries.

**3.** Beat milk and egg and yolk together in separate bowl. Make well in center of flour mixture and pour in milk mixture. Using rubber spatula, gently stir mixture, scraping from edges of bowl and folding inward until very shaggy dough forms and some bits of flour remain. Do not overmix.

**4.** Turn out dough onto well-floured counter and, if necessary, knead briefly until dough just comes together, about 3 turns. Using your floured hands and bench scraper, shape dough into 12 by 4-inch rectangle, about 1½ inches tall. Using knife or bench scraper, cut dough crosswise into 4 equal rectangles. Cut each rectangle diagonally into 2 triangles (you should have 8 scones total). Transfer scones to prepared sheet. Bake until scones are lightly golden on top, 16 to 18 minutes, rotating pan halfway through baking.

**5. for the glaze** While scones bake, combine melted butter and honey in small bowl.

**6.** Remove scones from oven and brush tops evenly with glaze mixture. Return scones to oven and continue to bake until golden brown on top, 5 to 8 minutes longer. Transfer scones to wire rack and let cool for at least 10 minutes before serving.

**to make ahead**
Unbaked scones can be frozen for several weeks. After cutting scones into triangles in step 4, freeze them on baking sheet. Transfer frozen scones to zipper-lock freezer bag. When ready to bake, heat oven to 375 degrees and extend cooking time in step 4 to 23 to 26 minutes. Glaze time in step 6 will remain at 5 to 8 minutes.

# british-style currant scones

*why this recipe works* Unlike their dense, rich American counterparts, British scones are light, fluffy affairs, a simple yet stately addition to brunch and perfect for pairing with butter and jam. To make sure these airy scones baked up tall, we created a fine, tender, cakey crumb by thoroughly integrating softened butter pieces into the dry ingredients using a food processor. A whopping 2 tablespoons of baking powder and lengthy, structure-building kneading guaranteed a high rise. Stamping out the scones with a sharp-edged cutter and being careful not to twist it also helped, encouraging each one to rise straight up as they baked. As a final stroke, we started the scones out in a hot 500-degree oven, the high heat encouraging an instant growth spurt as the water steamed and evaporated, but then we let them finish baking at a more moderate 425 degrees. Two touches that made these special scones even better: Tiny dried currants offered delicate bites of sweetness in each scone, and brushing the tops with a milk-egg wash enhanced browning. We prefer whole milk in this recipe, but low-fat milk can be used. The dough will be quite soft and wet; dust your work surface and your hands liberally with flour. For a tall, even rise, use a sharp-edged biscuit cutter and push straight down; do not twist the cutter. Serve scones with jam as well as salted butter or clotted cream.

*makes 12 scones*
*total time: 45 minutes*

3 cups (15 ounces)
all-purpose flour

⅓ cup (2⅓ ounces) sugar

2 tablespoons baking powder

½ teaspoon salt

8 tablespoons unsalted butter, cut into ½-inch pieces and softened

¾ cup dried currants

1 cup whole milk

2 large eggs

1. Adjust oven rack to upper-middle position and heat oven to 500 degrees. Line rimmed baking sheet with parchment paper. Pulse flour, sugar, baking powder, and salt in food processor until combined, about 5 pulses. Add butter and pulse until fully incorporated and mixture looks like very fine crumbs with no visible butter, about 20 pulses. Transfer mixture to large bowl and stir in currants.

2. Whisk milk and eggs together in second bowl. Set aside 2 tablespoons milk mixture. Add remaining milk mixture to flour mixture and, using rubber spatula, fold together until almost no dry bits of flour remain.

3. Transfer dough to well-floured counter and gather into ball. With your floured hands, knead until surface is smooth and free of cracks, 25 to 30 times. Press gently to form disk. Using floured rolling pin, roll disk into 9-inch round, about 1 inch thick. Using floured 2½-inch round cutter, stamp out 8 rounds, recoating cutter with flour if it begins to stick. Arrange scones on prepared sheet. Gather dough scraps, form into ball, and knead gently until surface is smooth. Roll dough to 1-inch thickness and stamp out 4 rounds. Discard remaining dough.

4. Brush tops of scones with reserved milk mixture. Reduce oven temperature to 425 degrees and bake scones until risen and golden brown, 10 to 12 minutes, rotating sheet halfway through baking. Transfer scones to wire rack and let cool for at least 10 minutes. Serve scones warm or at room temperature.

**to make ahead**
These scones are best served fresh, but leftover scones may be stored in freezer and reheated in 300-degree oven for 15 minutes before serving.

# cheddar biscuits

*why this recipe works*  Simple to make and rewardingly cheesy, these speedy cheddar biscuits are the perfect savory addition to your brunch bread basket. To keep the process quick and easy, we decided to use a cream biscuit base: Instead of cutting butter into flour, we simply poured rich heavy cream into the dry ingredients. Using flavor-packed cheddar meant our biscuits baked up cheesy, not greasy, and saving some cheese to sprinkle onto the biscuits partway through baking reinforced their rich taste without weighing them down. We made sure every last bit of flour made it into the rich biscuit dough by clearing out the bowl with some more cream and working the scraps into the rest of the dough. Brief kneading smoothed out the cheddar-filled ball, which we patted into a circle and sliced into generous wedges. These cheddar-laced biscuits emerged tender and flavorful, and they were so easy to make we had no qualms about coming up with a few more tasty variations. Bake the biscuits immediately after cutting them. Allowing the dough to sit for any length of time can decrease the leavening power of the baking powder and prevent the biscuits from rising properly in the oven.

*makes 8 biscuits*
*total time: 30 minutes*

2 cups (10 ounces) all-purpose flour

2 teaspoons sugar

2 teaspoons baking powder

½ teaspoon salt

3 ounces extra-sharp cheddar cheese, shredded (¾ cup)

1½ cups heavy cream

**1.** Adjust oven rack to upper-middle position and heat oven to 425 degrees. Line baking sheet with parchment paper.

**2.** Whisk flour, sugar, baking powder, and salt together in medium bowl. Stir in ½ cup cheddar. Add 1¼ cups cream and stir with wooden spoon until dough forms, about 30 seconds. Turn out dough onto counter, leaving dry, floury bits in bowl. Add remaining ¼ cup cream, 1 tablespoon at a time, to bowl, mixing with wooden spoon after each addition until dry bits are moistened. Add moistened bits to dough and knead by hand just until smooth, about 30 seconds.

**3.** Pat dough into 8-inch circle, cut into 8 wedges, and transfer to prepared sheet. Bake until wedges are just beginning to brown, 7 to 9 minutes. Remove sheet from oven, sprinkle each biscuit with 1½ teaspoons cheddar, rotate sheet, and return to oven. Bake until biscuits are golden brown and cheese topping has melted, 7 to 9 minutes. Serve warm.

## variations

### jalapeño-jack biscuits
Substitute pepper Jack for cheddar. Add 1 tablespoon finely chopped jalapeño, 1 tablespoon finely chopped chives, and ¼ teaspoon cayenne to flour mixture. Increase both baking times to 9 minutes.

### parmesan-garlic biscuits
Substitute 1 cup Parmesan for cheddar. Add ¾ cup Parmesan, 2 minced garlic cloves, and ½ teaspoon pepper to flour mixture and sprinkle remaining ¼ cup Parmesan over biscuits halfway through baking.

### swiss-caraway biscuits
Substitute 1 cup Swiss cheese for cheddar. Add ¾ cup Swiss cheese and 1 tablespoon toasted caraway seeds to flour mixture and sprinkle remaining ¼ cup Swiss cheese over biscuits halfway through baking.

# flaky buttermilk biscuits

*why this recipe works* These elegant biscuits come closer to pastry than dinner roll, with a golden crust concealing countless flaky, buttery layers. The secret lay in how we incorporated the butter: Rather than cut it into the flour, we pressed it into small pieces, then carefully folded the dough and sandwiched the butter into thin sheets between thin layers of flour. Brushed with butter, our biscuits baked up crisp, flaky, and decadent. The dough is sticky through the first set of folds. You will use up to 1 cup of flour dusting the counter, dough, and rolling pin. Be careful not to incorporate large pockets of flour into the dough when folding it. When cutting the biscuits, press down with firm, even pressure; do not twist the cutter.

*makes 12 biscuits*
*total time: 1 hour 15 minutes*

2½ cups (12½ ounces) all-purpose flour, plus extra for rolling and cutting biscuits

1 tablespoon baking powder

½ teaspoon baking soda

1 teaspoon salt

2 tablespoons vegetable shortening, cut into ½-inch chunks

8 tablespoons unsalted butter, chilled, lightly floured, and cut into ⅛-inch-thick slices, plus 2 tablespoons melted and cooled

1⅛–1¼ cups buttermilk, chilled

1. Adjust oven rack to lower-middle position and heat oven to 450 degrees. Whisk flour, baking powder, baking soda, and salt together in large bowl.

2. Add shortening to flour mixture; break up chunks with your fingertips until only small, pea-size pieces remain. Working with few butter slices at a time, drop butter slices into flour mixture and toss to coat. Pick up each butter slice and press between your well-floured fingertips into flat, nickel-size pieces. Repeat until all butter slices are incorporated, then toss to combine.

Freeze mixture in bowl until chilled, about 15 minutes, or refrigerate for about 30 minutes.

3. Spray 24-inch-square area of counter with vegetable oil spray; spread oil spray evenly across surface with clean dish towel or paper towel. Sprinkle ⅓ cup flour across counter, then gently spread flour across sprayed area with your palm to form thin, even coating. Add 1 cup plus 2 tablespoons buttermilk to flour mixture. Stir briskly with fork until ball forms and no dry bits of flour are visible, adding remaining 2 tablespoons buttermilk as needed (dough will be sticky and shaggy but should clear sides of bowl). With rubber spatula, transfer dough to center of prepared counter, dust surface lightly with flour, and, using your floured hands, form dough into cohesive ball.

4. Pat dough into approximate 10-inch square, then roll into 18 by 14-inch rectangle about ¼ inch thick, dusting dough and rolling pin with flour as needed. Use bench scraper or thin metal spatula to fold dough into thirds, brushing any excess flour from surface of dough. Lift short end of dough and fold into thirds again to form approximate 6 by 4-inch rectangle.

Rotate dough 90 degrees, dusting counter underneath with flour, then roll and fold dough again, dusting with flour as needed.

5. Roll dough into 10-inch square about ½ inch thick. Flip dough over and cut 9 rounds with floured 3-inch round cutter, dipping cutter back into flour after each cut. Carefully invert and transfer rounds to ungreased baking sheet, spacing them 1 inch apart. Gather dough scraps into ball and roll and fold once or twice until scraps form smooth dough. Roll dough into ½-inch-thick round and cut 3 more rounds and transfer to sheet. Discard excess dough.

6. Brush tops of rounds with melted butter. Bake, without opening oven door, until tops are golden brown and crisp, 15 to 17 minutes. Let biscuits cool on sheet for 5 to 10 minutes before serving.

### variation

flaky buttermilk biscuits with parmesan
Add ¼ cup finely grated Parmesan cheese, ¼ teaspoon pepper, and ⅛ teaspoon cayenne pepper to flour mixture in step 1. Sprinkle dough rounds with another ¼ cup finely grated Parmesan after brushing with melted butter in step 6.

# popovers

*why this recipe works* These foolproof popovers soar to towering heights as if by magic, delivering a crisp exterior and an airy, custardy interior. To bake crisp, substantial, structurally sound popovers that climbed high out of the deep wells of the popover tin, we called on high-protein bread flour. Whisking milk and plenty of melted butter into the flour and letting it rest before baking relaxed the proteins and prevented the popovers from setting up too quickly for an even rise. Whole milk is traditional, but the fat weighed down our batter. Switching to low-fat milk and cutting the amount of melted butter from 4 tablespoons to 3 lightened it up for more dramatic lift while still keeping the popovers' flavor rich. Starting the popovers in a hot oven before dropping the temperature to finish encouraged a strong initial rise and deep crisping while also allowing the interiors to finish baking on pace with the exteriors. Trapped steam can cause popovers to collapse and lose their crispness, so we poked a hole in the top of each popover toward the end of baking and again while cooling to allow steam to escape. Greasing the popover pan with shortening ensures the best release, but vegetable oil spray may be substituted; do not use butter. To monitor the popovers' progress without opening the oven door, use the oven light.

*makes 6 popovers*
*total time: 1 hour 30 minutes*
*(plus 1 hour resting time)*

Shortening

2 cups (11 ounces) bread flour, plus extra for pan

3 large eggs, room temperature

2 cups warm 1 or 2 percent low-fat milk (110 degrees)

3 tablespoons unsalted butter, melted

1 teaspoon sugar

1 teaspoon salt

**1.** Grease 6-cup popover pan with shortening, then flour pan lightly. Whisk eggs in medium bowl until light and foamy. Slowly whisk in warm milk, melted butter, and sugar until incorporated.

**2.** Whisk flour and salt together in large bowl. Whisk three-quarters of milk mixture into flour mixture until no lumps remain, then whisk in remaining milk mixture.

**3.** Transfer batter to 4-cup liquid measuring cup, cover tightly with plastic wrap, and let rest for at least 1 hour.

**4.** Adjust oven rack to lower-middle position and heat oven to 450 degrees. Whisk batter to recombine, then pour into prepared pan (batter will not reach top of cups). Bake until just beginning to brown, about 20 minutes.

**5.** Without opening oven door, reduce oven temperature to 300 degrees and continue to bake until popovers are golden brown, 35 to 40 minutes.

**6.** Poke small hole in top of each popover with skewer and continue to bake until deep golden brown, about 10 minutes. Transfer pan to wire rack, poke popovers again with skewer, and let cool for 2 minutes. Remove popovers from pan and serve warm.

### to make ahead
Batter, prepared through step 3, can be refrigerated for up to 24 hours; to bake, let sit at room temperature for 1 hour and continue with step 4. Baked popovers can be stored at room temperature for up to 2 days; to reheat, bake on rimmed baking sheet in 400-degree oven for 5 to 8 minutes until warmed through.

# muffin tin doughnuts

*why this recipe works* This recipe delivers the best of both worlds: the sweet, satisfying crispness and tender crumb of a cake doughnut and the effortless ease of an everyday muffin. Baking muffins rich and crisp enough to be mistaken for a doughnut all came down to one ingredient: butter. A full stick of melted butter along with an extra egg yolk gave us indulgent, moist muffins, and cutting the flour with cornstarch delivered a perfectly tender crumb that wouldn't break apart. Baking the muffins in a hot oven created just the right crust, but the pièce de résistance was the crunchy cinnamon-sugar coating. After brushing each muffin in more melted butter, we rolled them in the sweet, spiced coating and allowed them to cool before digging in. From crust to crumb, these muffins were every inch the doughnuts in disguise we craved. In step 3, brush the doughnuts generously, using up all the melted butter. Use your hand to press the cinnamon sugar onto the doughnuts to coat them completely.

*makes 12 doughnuts*
*total time: 1 hour*

*doughnuts*
2¾ cups (13¾ ounces) all-purpose flour

1 cup (7 ounces) sugar

¼ cup cornstarch

1 tablespoon baking powder

1 teaspoon salt

½ teaspoon ground nutmeg

1 cup buttermilk

8 tablespoons unsalted butter, melted

2 large eggs plus 1 large yolk

*coating*
1 cup sugar

2 teaspoons ground cinnamon

8 tablespoons unsalted butter, melted

**1. for the doughnuts** Adjust oven rack to middle position and heat oven to 400 degrees. Spray 12-cup muffin tin with vegetable oil spray. Whisk flour, sugar, cornstarch, baking powder, salt, and nutmeg together in bowl. Whisk buttermilk, melted butter, and eggs and yolk together in separate bowl. Add wet ingredients to dry ingredients and stir with rubber spatula until just combined.

**2.** Divide batter evenly among prepared muffin cups. Bake until doughnuts are lightly browned and toothpick inserted in center comes out clean, 19 to 22 minutes, rotating muffin tin halfway through baking. Let doughnuts cool in tin for 5 minutes.

**3. for the coating** Whisk sugar and cinnamon together in bowl. Remove doughnuts from tin. Working with 1 doughnut at a time, brush all over with melted butter, then roll in cinnamon sugar, pressing lightly to adhere. Transfer to wire rack and let cool for 15 minutes. Serve.

# apple fritters

*why this recipe works* Apple fritters offer a sweet, fruity counterpoint to savory brunch entrées, and ours outshine the best of the doughnut shop because they're crisp on the outside, moist on the inside, and sing out pure apple flavor. To keep the fritters light and moist (not wet), we banned excess moisture from the apples by cutting them into small cubes, patting them dry with paper towels, and tossing them with the dry ingredients so the flour, sugar, baking powder, and spices could sop up some of the juices. We used apple cider instead of milk in our batter because it reinforced the apple taste, and we called on warm, aromatic cinnamon and nutmeg for even more complementary flavor. Flattening portions of batter in the hot oil enabled the fritters to cook through without overbrowning. To finish, we spooned on a cider-spiked glaze for one final layer of apple-imbued flavor. We like to use Granny Smith apples in these fritters because they are tart and crisp. We add apple cider to both the batter and the glaze to provide strong apple flavor in our fritters; don't be tempted to substitute apple juice for the cider, as the juice will not provide enough flavor.

*makes 10 fritters*
*total time: 1 hour*

### fritters
2 Granny Smith apples, peeled, cored, halved, and cut into ¼-inch pieces

2 cups (10 ounces) all-purpose flour

⅓ cup (2⅓ ounces) granulated sugar

1 tablespoon baking powder

1 teaspoon salt

1 teaspoon ground cinnamon

¼ teaspoon ground nutmeg

¾ cup apple cider

2 large eggs, lightly beaten

2 tablespoons unsalted butter, melted

3 cups peanut or vegetable oil

### glaze
2 cups (8 ounces) confectioners' sugar

¼ cup apple cider

½ teaspoon ground cinnamon

¼ teaspoon ground nutmeg

**1. for the fritters** Spread apples in single layer on paper towel–lined rimmed baking sheet and pat dry thoroughly with paper towels. Whisk flour, sugar, baking powder, salt, cinnamon, and nutmeg together in large bowl. Whisk cider, eggs, and melted butter in medium bowl until combined. Stir apples into flour mixture until incorporated. Stir in cider mixture until combined.

**2.** Set wire rack in rimmed baking sheet. Heat oil in Dutch oven over medium-high heat to 350 degrees. Using ⅓-cup dry measuring cup and spoon, carefully place 5 heaping portions of batter in oil. Using back of spoon, press batter lightly to flatten. Fry, adjusting burner if necessary to maintain oil temperature between 325 and 350 degrees, until fritters are deep golden brown, 2 to 3 minutes per side. Transfer to prepared wire rack. Return oil to 350 degrees and repeat with remaining batter. Let fritters cool for 5 minutes.

**3. for the glaze** While fritters cool, whisk all ingredients in medium bowl until smooth. Top each fritter with 1 heaping tablespoon glaze. Let glaze set for 10 minutes before serving.

# morning buns

*why this recipe works* Combine the rich layers of a croissant with the sweet swirls of a cinnamon bun and you'll have one of our favorite brunch pastries: morning buns. For a simpler route to a yeasted, croissant-like pastry, we added a packet of yeast to a quick puff pastry dough. We created long, thin pieces of flake-producing butter by adding chilled butter to the dry ingredients in a zipper-lock bag and rolling over it with a rolling pin. Orange zest and juice offered sweet, citrusy brightness. We started our rolls in a hot oven for a rapid rise but later dropped the temperature to impart gradual, even browning. If the dough becomes too soft to work with at any point, refrigerate it until it's firm enough to easily handle.

*makes 12 buns*
*total time: 1 hour 30 minutes*
*(plus 1 hour 15 minutes to*
*1 hour 45 minutes freezing*
*and rising time)*

*dough*
**3 cups (15 ounces)**
**all-purpose flour**

**1 tablespoon granulated sugar**

**2¼ teaspoons instant or**
**rapid-rise yeast**

**¾ teaspoon salt**

**24 tablespoons (3 sticks)**
**unsalted butter, cut into**
**¼-inch slices and chilled**

**1 cup sour cream, chilled**

**¼ cup orange juice, chilled**

**3 tablespoons ice water**

**1 large egg yolk**

*filling*
**½ cup (3½ ounces) granulated**
**sugar**

**½ cup packed (3½ ounces) light**
**brown sugar**

**1 tablespoon grated orange zest**

**2 teaspoons ground cinnamon**

**1 teaspoon vanilla extract**

**1. for the dough** Combine flour, sugar, yeast, and salt in 1-gallon zipper-lock bag. Add butter to bag, seal, and shake to coat. Press air out of bag and reseal. Roll over bag several times with rolling pin, shaking bag after each roll, until butter is pressed into large flakes.

**2.** Transfer mixture to large bowl and stir in sour cream, orange juice, ice water, and egg yolk with wooden spoon until combined. Transfer dough to lightly floured counter and knead by hand to form smooth, round ball, about 30 seconds.

**3.** Press and roll dough into 20 by 12-inch rectangle, with short side parallel to counter edge. Roll dough away from you into firm cylinder, keeping roll taut by tucking it under itself as you go.

**4.** With seam side down, flatten cylinder into 12 by 4-inch rectangle. Transfer to parchment paper–lined rimmed baking sheet, cover loosely with greased plastic wrap, and freeze for 15 minutes.

**5. for the filling** Line 12-cup muffin tin with paper or foil liners and spray with vegetable oil spray. Combine all ingredients in bowl. Transfer dough to lightly floured counter and roll into 20 by 12-inch rectangle, with long side parallel to counter edge. Sprinkle with sugar mixture, leaving ½-inch border around edges, and press lightly to adhere.

**6.** Roll dough away from you into firm cylinder, keeping roll taut by tucking it under itself as you go. Pinch seam closed, then reshape cylinder as needed to be 20 inches in length with uniform thickness.

**7.** Using serrated knife, trim ½ inch dough from each end and discard. Cut cylinder into 12 pieces and place cut side up in muffin cups. Cover loosely with greased plastic and let rise until doubled in size, 1 to 1½ hours.

**8.** Adjust oven rack to middle position and heat oven to 425 degrees. Bake until buns begin to rise, about 5 minutes, then reduce oven temperature to 325 degrees. Continue to bake until buns are deep golden brown, 40 to 50 minutes, rotating muffin tin halfway through baking. Let buns cool in muffin tin for 5 minutes, then transfer to wire rack and discard liners. Serve warm.

**to make ahead**
Unrisen buns can be refrigerated for at least 16 hours or up to 24 hours; let buns sit at room temperature for 1 hour before baking.

# ultimate cinnamon buns

*why this recipe works* These sinfully good cinnamon buns are pure indulgence. We achieved a soft, tender dough by cutting all-purpose flour with cornstarch, and a layer of butter sprinkled with cinnamon and brown sugar produced a rich, gooey filling. Our thick, tangy cream cheese glaze put these buns over the top. We do not recommend mixing this dough by hand.

*makes 8 buns*
*total time: 2 hours*
*(plus 3 to 3 hours 30 minutes*
*rising time)*

*dough*
**4¼ cups (21¼ ounces) all-purpose flour**

**½ cup (2 ounces) cornstarch**

**2¼ teaspoons instant or rapid-rise yeast**

**1½ teaspoons salt**

**¾ cup whole milk, room temperature**

**3 large eggs, room temperature**

**½ cup (3½ ounces) granulated sugar**

**12 tablespoons unsalted butter, softened**

*filling*
**1½ cups packed (10½ ounces) light brown sugar**

**1½ tablespoons ground cinnamon**

**¼ teaspoon salt**

**4 tablespoons unsalted butter, softened**

*glaze*
**1½ cups (6 ounces) confectioners' sugar**

**4 ounces cream cheese, softened**

**1 tablespoon whole milk**

**1 teaspoon vanilla extract**

**1. for the dough** Whisk flour, cornstarch, yeast, and salt together in bowl of stand mixer.

Whisk milk, eggs, and sugar in 4-cup liquid measuring cup until sugar has dissolved.

**2.** Using dough hook on low speed, slowly add milk mixture to flour mixture and mix until cohesive dough starts to form and no dry flour remains, about 2 minutes, scraping down bowl as needed. Increase speed to medium-low, add butter, 1 tablespoon at a time, and knead until butter is fully incorporated, about 6 minutes. Continue to knead until dough is smooth and elastic and clears sides of bowl, about 3 minutes.

**3.** Transfer dough to lightly floured counter and knead by hand to form smooth, round ball, about 30 seconds. Place dough seam side down in lightly greased large bowl or container, cover tightly with plastic wrap, and let rise until doubled in size, 2 to 2½ hours.

**4.** Make foil sling for 13 by 9-inch baking pan by folding 2 long sheets of aluminum foil; first sheet should be 13 inches wide and second sheet should be 9 inches wide. Lay sheets of foil in pan perpendicular to each other, with extra foil hanging over edges of pan. Push foil into corners and up sides of pan, smoothing foil flush to pan, then spray foil with vegetable oil spray.

**5. for the filling** Combine sugar, cinnamon, and salt in bowl. Press down on dough to deflate, then transfer to lightly floured counter. Press and roll dough into 18-inch square. Spread butter over dough, leaving ½-inch border around edges. Sprinkle with sugar mixture, leaving ¾-inch border at top edge, and press lightly to adhere.

**6.** Roll dough away from you into firm cylinder, keeping roll taut by tucking it under itself as you go. Pinch seam closed, then reshape cylinder as needed to be 18 inches in length with uniform thickness. Using serrated knife, cut cylinder into 8 pieces and arrange cut side down in prepared pan. Cover loosely with greased plastic and let rise until doubled in size, about 1 hour.

**7.** Adjust oven rack to middle position and heat oven to 350 degrees. Bake until buns are golden brown and filling is melted, 35 to 40 minutes, rotating pan halfway through baking.

**8. for the glaze** Whisk all ingredients in bowl until smooth. Top buns with ½ cup glaze and let cool in pan for 30 minutes. Using foil overhang, transfer buns to wire rack and top with remaining glaze. Serve warm.

**to make ahead**
Unrisen buns can be refrigerated for at least 16 hours or up to 24 hours; let buns sit at room temperature for 1 hour before baking.

# monkey bread

*why this recipe works* Comprised of tempting caramelized balls of dough baked in a Bundt pan, monkey bread is the perfect pull-apart sweet to snack on at the start of a laid-back brunch. Rather than rely on convenient but bland store-bought biscuit dough, we prepared a rich, sweet dough from scratch and expedited its proofing by using plenty of instant yeast. Rolling the dough into balls and coating them in melted butter and a mixture of brown sugar and cinnamon gave them a caramel-like coating as the bread baked. Do not leave the bread in the pan for more than 5 minutes after baking, or it will stick.

*makes 1 loaf*
*total time: 2 hours*
*(plus 3 to 4 hours rising time)*

*dough*
3¼ cups (16¼ ounces) all-purpose flour

2¼ teaspoons instant or rapid-rise yeast

2 teaspoons salt

1 cup whole milk, room temperature

⅓ cup water, room temperature

¼ cup (1¾ ounces) granulated sugar

2 tablespoons unsalted butter, melted

*brown sugar coating*
1 cup packed (7 ounces) light brown sugar

2 teaspoons ground cinnamon

8 tablespoons unsalted butter, melted and cooled

*glaze*
1 cup (4 ounces) confectioners' sugar

2 tablespoons whole milk

**1. for the dough** Whisk flour, yeast, and salt together in bowl of stand mixer. Whisk milk, water, sugar, and melted butter in 4-cup liquid measuring cup until sugar has dissolved. Using dough hook on low speed, slowly add milk mixture to flour mixture and mix until cohesive dough starts to form and no dry flour remains, about 2 minutes, scraping down bowl as needed. Increase speed to medium-low and knead until dough is smooth and elastic and clears sides of bowl but sticks to bottom, 8 to 10 minutes.

**2.** Transfer dough to lightly floured counter and knead by hand to form smooth, round ball, about 30 seconds. Place dough seam side down in lightly greased large bowl or container, cover tightly with plastic wrap, and let rise until doubled in size, 1½ to 2 hours.

**3. for the brown sugar coating** Thoroughly grease 12-cup nonstick Bundt pan. Combine sugar and cinnamon in medium bowl. Place melted butter in second bowl.

**4.** Transfer dough to lightly floured counter and press into rough 8-inch square. Using pizza cutter or chef's knife, cut dough into 8 even strips. Cut each strip into 8 pieces (64 pieces total). Cover loosely with greased plastic.

**5.** Working with a few pieces of dough at a time (keep remaining pieces covered), place on clean counter and, using your cupped hand, drag in small circles until dough feels taut and round. Dip balls in melted butter, then roll in sugar mixture to coat. Place balls in prepared pan, staggering seams where dough balls meet as you build layers.

**6.** Cover pan tightly with plastic and let rise until dough balls reach 1 to 2 inches below lip of pan, 1½ to 2 hours.

**7.** Adjust oven rack to middle position and heat oven to 350 degrees. Bake until top is deep golden brown and caramel begins to bubble around edges, 30 to 35 minutes, rotating pan halfway through baking. Let bread cool in pan for 5 minutes, then invert onto serving platter and let cool for 10 minutes.

**8. for the glaze** Meanwhile, whisk sugar and milk in bowl until smooth. Drizzle glaze over bread, letting it run down sides. Serve warm.

### to make ahead
Unrisen dough can be refrigerated for at least 8 hours or up to 16 hours; let sit at room temperature for 1 hour before shaping in step 4.

# ultimate banana bread

*why this recipe works*  This banana bread puts all others to shame because it harnesses maximum banana flavor while still delivering a tender, moist (not soggy) brunch bread. The secret behind bringing as many bananas into play as possible? Moisture management. We microwaved five bananas to concentrate their flavor and drain off their juices, but rather than let the juices go to waste, we reduced them into a concentrated banana syrup. Mashed in with the spent bananas, melted butter, an egg, light brown sugar, and vanilla, this syrup imparted enormous banana taste to put the loaf's flavor right over the top. To add some extra embellishment, we sliced a sixth banana and shingled it on top of the unbaked loaf. Adding a sprinkling of sugar created an enticingly caramelized crust. It is important to use extremely ripe, heavily speckled (or even black) bananas in this recipe. This recipe can be made using five thawed frozen bananas; since thawed frozen bananas release a large amount of liquid naturally, they can bypass the 5 or so minutes of microwaving in step 2 and go directly into the fine-mesh strainer. Do not use a thawed frozen banana in step 4; it will be too soft to neatly slice. Instead, if you don't have a very ripe large banana on hand, skip adding the banana slices and simply sprinkle the top of the banana bread with sugar. The test kitchen's preferred loaf pan measures 8½ by 4½ inches; if you use a 9 by 5-inch loaf pan, start checking for doneness 5 minutes early.

*makes 1 loaf*
*total time: 1 hour 45 minutes*
*to 2 hours*
*(plus 1 hour cooling time)*

1¾ cups (8¾ ounces)
all-purpose flour

1 teaspoon baking soda

½ teaspoon salt

6 very ripe large bananas
(2¼ pounds), peeled

8 tablespoons unsalted butter,
melted and cooled

2 large eggs

¾ cup packed (5¼ ounces) light
brown sugar

1 teaspoon vanilla extract

½ cup walnuts, toasted and
chopped coarse (optional)

2 teaspoons granulated sugar

1. Adjust oven rack to middle position and heat oven to 350 degrees. Spray 8½ by 4½-inch loaf pan with vegetable oil spray. Whisk flour, baking soda, and salt together in large bowl; set aside.

2. Place 5 bananas in separate bowl, cover, and microwave until bananas are soft and have released liquid, about 5 minutes. Transfer bananas to fine-mesh strainer set over medium bowl and let drain, stirring occasionally, for 15 minutes (you should have between ½ and ¾ cup liquid).

3. Transfer liquid to medium saucepan and cook over medium-high heat until reduced to ¼ cup, about 5 minutes. Return drained bananas to bowl. Off heat, stir reduced liquid into bananas and mash with potato masher until mostly smooth. Whisk in melted butter, eggs, brown sugar, and vanilla.

4. Pour banana mixture into flour mixture and stir until just combined, with some streaks of flour remaining. Gently fold in walnuts, if using. Transfer batter to prepared pan. Slice remaining banana on bias ¼ inch thick. Shingle banana slices on top of loaf in 2 rows, leaving 1½-inch-wide space down center to ensure even rise. Sprinkle granulated sugar evenly over loaf.

5. Bake until toothpick inserted in center of loaf comes out clean, 55 minutes to 1¼ hours, rotating pan halfway through baking. Let loaf cool in pan for 10 minutes, then remove loaf from pan and let cool on wire rack for 1 hour before serving.

**to make ahead**
Cooled bread can be stored at room temperature, covered tightly with plastic wrap, for up to 3 days.

# irish brown soda bread

*why this recipe works* Irish brown soda bread is a hearty, wholesome loaf that tastes as good with a helping of scrambled eggs as it does with a smear of salted butter or tangy marmalade. And not only is this humble bread versatile, it's also simple to prepare. We mimicked the wheaty, nutty flavor and rustic crumb imparted by hard-to-find Irish wholemeal flour by combining whole-wheat flour with wheat bran and wheat germ. Cutting this mixture with all-purpose flour and a touch of sugar helped balance out the strong wheat flavor. The addition of baking powder guaranteed a nicely risen loaf, but we also included baking soda for added browning and the characteristic mineral tang we love in soda breads. Acidic buttermilk contributed even more tangy flavor. Finally, to force the soft dough to rise upward rather than outward, we baked our bread in a cake pan. Our favorite whole-wheat flour is King Arthur Premium. To ensure the best flavor, use fresh whole-wheat flour. Wheat bran can be found at natural foods stores or in the baking aisle of your supermarket.

*makes 1 loaf*
*total time: 1 hour*
*(plus 1 hour cooling time)*

2 cups (11 ounces)
**whole-wheat flour**

1 cup (5 ounces)
**all-purpose flour**

1 cup **wheat bran**

¼ cup **wheat germ**

2 teaspoons **sugar**

1½ teaspoons **baking powder**

1½ teaspoons **baking soda**

1 teaspoon **salt**

2 cups **buttermilk**

1. Adjust oven rack to middle position and heat oven to 375 degrees. Lightly grease 8-inch round cake pan. Whisk whole-wheat flour, all-purpose flour, wheat bran, wheat germ, sugar, baking powder, baking soda, and salt together in medium bowl.

2. Add buttermilk and stir with rubber spatula until all flour is moistened and dough forms soft, ragged mass. Transfer dough to counter and gently shape into 6-inch round (surface will be craggy). Using serrated knife, cut ½-inch-deep cross about 5 inches long on top of loaf. Transfer to prepared pan. Bake until loaf is lightly browned and center registers 185 degrees, 40 to 45 minutes, rotating pan halfway through baking.

3. Invert loaf onto wire rack. Reinvert loaf and let cool for at least 1 hour. Slice and serve.

**to make ahead**
This bread is best when served on the day it is made, but leftovers can be wrapped in plastic wrap and stored at room temperature for up to 2 days.

# pumpkin bread

*why this recipe works* This pumpkin loaf may be a quick bread, but with its sweetly spiced flavor, moist, tender crumb, and satisfyingly crunchy bites of walnut and streusel, it still has plenty of panache. To coax clear pumpkin flavor out of convenient canned puree, we started out on the stovetop. Cooking the puree over medium heat along with the warm, complementary flavors of cinnamon, nutmeg, and cloves lightly caramelized the pumpkin, deepening and concentrating its flavor. We sweetened the mixture with granulated sugar as well as the nuanced caramel notes of brown sugar. We often spread tangy cream cheese onto pumpkin bread, but for this recipe we decided to stir it right into the batter, melting small cubes into the hot puree as it cooled. This gave our loaves an added creamy dimension, and a hit of buttermilk doubled down on the cream cheese's appealing tang. Toasted nuts offered textural contrast, as did a simple streusel topping sprinkled on before baking. This recipe yields two loaves of bread. The test kitchen's preferred loaf pan measures 8½ by 4½ inches; if using a 9 by 5-inch loaf pan, start checking for doneness 5 minutes early.

*makes 2 loaves*
*total time: 1 hour 30 minutes*
*(plus 1 hour 50 minutes*
*cooling time)*

*topping*
**5 tablespoons packed
(2¼ ounces) light brown sugar**

**1 tablespoon all-purpose flour**

**1 tablespoon unsalted butter,
softened**

**1 teaspoon ground cinnamon**

**⅛ teaspoon salt**

*bread*
**2 cups (10 ounces)
all-purpose flour**

**1½ teaspoons baking powder**

**½ teaspoon baking soda**

**1 (15-ounce) can unsweetened
pumpkin puree**

**1½ teaspoons ground cinnamon**

**1 teaspoon salt**

**¼ teaspoon ground nutmeg**

**⅛ teaspoon ground cloves**

**1 cup (7 ounces) granulated sugar**

**1 cup packed (7 ounces) light
brown sugar**

**½ cup vegetable oil**

**4 ounces cream cheese,
cut into 12 pieces**

**4 large eggs**

**¼ cup buttermilk**

**1 cup walnuts, toasted and
chopped fine**

**1. for the topping** Using your fingers, mix all ingredients in bowl until well combined and topping resembles wet sand; set aside.

**2. for the bread** Adjust oven rack to middle position and heat oven to 350 degrees. Grease two 8½ by 4½-inch loaf pans. Whisk flour, baking powder, and baking soda together in bowl.

**3.** Combine pumpkin, cinnamon, salt, nutmeg, and cloves in large saucepan and cook over medium heat, stirring constantly, until reduced to 1½ cups, 6 to 8 minutes. Off heat, stir in granulated sugar, brown sugar, oil, and cream cheese until combined. Let mixture stand

for 5 minutes. Whisk until no visible pieces of cream cheese remain and mixture is homogeneous.

**4.** Whisk eggs and buttermilk together in bowl. Add egg mixture to pumpkin mixture and whisk to combine. Fold flour mixture into pumpkin mixture until combined (some small lumps of flour are OK). Fold walnuts into batter.

**5.** Transfer batter to prepared pans. Sprinkle topping evenly over top of each loaf. Bake until skewer inserted in center of loaf comes out clean, 45 to 50 minutes, rotating pans halfway through baking. Let loaves cool in pans on wire rack for 20 minutes. Remove loaves from pans and let cool on rack for at least 1½ hours. Serve warm or at room temperature.

**variation**

**pumpkin bread with
candied ginger**
Substitute ½ teaspoon ground ginger for cinnamon in topping. Fold ⅓ cup minced crystallized ginger into batter after flour mixture has been added in step 4.

# quick cheese bread

*why this recipe works* If you tend to pass up brunch sweets for something cheesy and savory, this effortless cheese bread is the recipe for you. We created a hearty, rich quick bread by folding the dry and wet ingredients together, incorporating small chunks of extra-sharp cheddar into the dough for indulgent pockets of rich, salty flavor throughout. A sprinkling of Parmesan into the bottom of the empty pan and another helping over the top of the loaf ensured a cheesy, salty crust. Use the large holes of a box grater to shred the Parmesan. You can substitute a mild (not aged) Asiago, crumbled into ¼- to ½-inch pieces, for the cheddar. The test kitchen's preferred loaf pan measures 8½ by 4½ inches; if you use a 9 by 5-inch loaf pan, start checking for doneness 5 minutes early. If, when testing the bread for doneness, the skewer comes out with what looks like uncooked batter clinging to it, try again in a different spot. (A skewer hitting a pocket of cheese may give a false indication.) The texture of the bread improves as it cools, so wait at least 45 minutes to slice into the loaf (it will take 3 hours for the loaf to cool entirely).

*makes 1 loaf*
*total time: 1 hour 30 minutes*
*(plus 45 minutes to 3 hours*
*cooling time)*

3 ounces Parmesan cheese, shredded (1 cup)

2½ cups (12½ ounces) all-purpose flour

1 tablespoon baking powder

1 teaspoon salt

⅛ teaspoon pepper

⅛ teaspoon cayenne pepper

4 ounces extra-sharp cheddar cheese, cut into ½-inch pieces (1 cup)

1 cup whole milk

½ cup sour cream

3 tablespoons unsalted butter, melted

1 large egg

**1.** Adjust oven rack to middle position and heat oven to 350 degrees. Grease 8½ by 4½-inch loaf pan, then sprinkle ½ cup Parmesan evenly in bottom of pan.

**2.** Whisk flour, baking powder, salt, pepper, and cayenne together in large bowl. Using rubber spatula, stir in cheddar, breaking up clumps, until cheese is coated with flour. Whisk milk, sour cream, melted butter, and egg together in medium bowl. Gently fold milk mixture into flour mixture until just combined (batter will be heavy and thick; do not overmix). Transfer batter to prepared pan; spread to sides of pan and smooth top with rubber spatula. Sprinkle remaining ½ cup Parmesan evenly over surface.

**3.** Bake until deep golden brown and skewer inserted in center comes out clean, 45 to 50 minutes, rotating pan halfway through baking. Let loaf cool in pan for 5 minutes. Remove loaf from pan and let cool on wire rack for at least 45 minutes before serving.

### variation

quick cheese bread with bacon, onion, and gruyère

Cook 5 slices bacon, cut into ½-inch pieces, in 10-inch nonstick skillet over medium heat until crispy, 5 to 7 minutes. Using slotted spoon, transfer bacon to paper towel–lined plate. Pour off all but 3 tablespoons fat from skillet. Add ½ cup finely chopped onion to fat left in skillet and cook over medium heat until softened, about 3 minutes; set aside. Substitute Gruyère cheese for cheddar and omit butter. Add bacon and onion to flour mixture with cheese in step 2.

### to make ahead

Wrap cooled loaf tightly with double layer of aluminum foil and freeze for up to 3 months. To reheat, bake frozen, wrapped loaf on middle rack in 375-degree oven until loaf yields under gentle pressure, 8 to 10 minutes. Remove foil and return bread to oven for five minutes to crisp exterior. Let cool for 15 minutes before serving.

# cranberry-nut bread

*why this recipe works* This cranberry-nut loaf falls somewhere between dense breakfast bread and light, airy cake and although its flavors seem tailor-made for the holidays, its sweet-tart balance and moist texture are perfectly suited to any special brunch. Using the standard quick-bread method of mixing—in which liquid and dry ingredients are mixed separately and then stirred together—helped us keep the texture perfectly dense and moist, while a combination of leaveners provided just the right amount of lift. Baking soda supported the structure and promoted browning, while baking powder enhanced the flavor. Rather than try to tamp down the cranberries' tartness with a lot of sugar, we held back, using just 1 cup sugar to 1½ cups cranberries for a loaf with balanced sweetness. A handful of toasted pecans added textural interest and toasty flavor and, to counter the berries' tart pop with citrusy brightness, we stirred orange juice and zest in with the liquid ingredients. Fresh or frozen cranberries (not thawed) will work here. The test kitchen's preferred loaf pan measures 8½ by 4½ inches; if you use a 9 by 5-inch loaf pan, start checking for doneness 5 minutes early.

*makes 1 loaf*
*total time: 1 hour 30 minutes*
*(plus 1 hour cooling time)*

⅔ cup buttermilk

6 tablespoons unsalted butter, melted and cooled

1 tablespoon grated orange zest plus ⅓ cup juice

1 large egg

2 cups (10 ounces) all-purpose flour

1 cup (7 ounces) sugar

1 teaspoon salt

1 teaspoon baking powder

¼ teaspoon baking soda

6 ounces (1½ cups) fresh or frozen cranberries, chopped coarse

½ cup pecans or walnuts, toasted and chopped coarse

1. Adjust oven rack to middle position and heat oven to 350 degrees. Grease 8½ by 4½-inch loaf pan. Stir buttermilk, melted butter, orange zest and juice, and egg together in bowl. In large bowl, whisk flour, sugar, salt, baking powder, and baking soda together. Stir buttermilk mixture into flour mixture with rubber spatula until just moistened. Gently stir in cranberries and pecans; do not overmix.

2. Scrape batter into prepared loaf pan and smooth top. Bake until golden brown and skewer inserted in center comes out clean, 55 minutes to 1¼ hours, rotating pan halfway through baking. Let loaf cool in pan for 10 minutes, then turn out onto wire rack and let cool for 1 hour before serving.

# english muffin bread

*why this recipe works* This singular loaf of bread delivers all the qualities we love about classic English muffins—their chewy interior, crunchy crust, and countless butter-thirsty crannies—but without any of the fussy kneading, rolling, cutting, or griddling. We re-created the distinct texture by using protein-rich bread flour, which created a chewy yet light consistency, and baking soda for the all-important coarse, honeycombed texture. Stirring heated milk into the dry ingredients activated the yeast and shortened the dough's proofing time. After mixing the no-knead dough, letting it rise, and baking it in cornmeal-lined loaf pans, we were rewarded with two loaves of nook-and-cranny–packed bread bursting with yeasty flavor and surrounded by a beautifully browned crust. Toasted to a speckled brown, this simple bread soaked up butter with abandon and tasted better than any store-bought muffins we'd ever tried. The test kitchen's preferred loaf pan measures 8½ by 4½ inches; if you use a 9 by 5-inch loaf pan, start checking for doneness 5 minutes early. This recipe yields two loaves of bread. Serve this bread with butter and jam.

*makes 2 loaves*
*total time: 45 minutes*
*(plus 2 hours rising and*
*cooling time)*

Cornmeal

**5 cups (27½ ounces) bread flour**

**1½ tablespoons instant or rapid-rise yeast**

**1 tablespoon sugar**

**2 teaspoons salt**

**1 teaspoon baking soda**

**3 cups whole milk, heated to 120 degrees**

**1.** Grease two 8½ by 4½-inch loaf pans and dust with cornmeal. Combine flour, yeast, sugar, salt, and baking soda in large bowl. Stir in hot milk until combined, about 1 minute. Cover dough with greased plastic wrap and let rise in warm place for 30 minutes, or until dough is bubbly and has doubled.

**2.** Stir dough and divide between prepared loaf pans, pushing into corners with greased rubber spatula. (Pans should be about two-thirds full.) Cover pans with greased plastic and let dough rise in warm place until it reaches edges of pans, about 30 minutes. Adjust oven rack to middle position and heat oven to 375 degrees.

**3.** Discard plastic and transfer pans to oven. Bake until loaves are well browned and register 200 degrees, about 30 minutes, rotating and switching pans halfway through baking. Turn loaves out onto wire rack and let cool completely, about 1 hour. Slice, toast, and serve.

# quick coffee cake

*why this recipe works* Tender, sweet, and, best of all, speedy, this recipe yields two tender cinnamon-spiced cakes that can be pulled together ahead of time and baked straight from the fridge or freezer. Cinnamon and equal parts brown and granulated sugars offered balanced sweetness and warmth while sour cream kept the cake moist and rich. Do not try to put all the batter into one large cake pan; it will bake unevenly. Drizzle cakes with Cream Cheese Glaze (recipe follows), if desired.

*makes 2 cakes*
*total time: 45 minutes*
*(plus 15 minutes cooling time)*

*topping*

⅓ cup packed (2⅓ ounces) light brown sugar

⅓ cup (2⅓ ounces) granulated sugar

⅓ cup (1⅔ ounces) all-purpose flour

4 tablespoons unsalted butter, softened

1 tablespoon ground cinnamon

1 cup pecans or walnuts, chopped coarse

*cake*

3 cups (15 ounces) all-purpose flour

1 tablespoon baking powder

1 teaspoon baking soda

1 teaspoon ground cinnamon

¼ teaspoon salt

1¾ cups sour cream

1 cup packed (7 ounces) light brown sugar

1 cup (7 ounces) granulated sugar

3 large eggs

7 tablespoons unsalted butter, melted and cooled

1. Adjust oven rack to middle position and heat oven to 350 degrees. Grease two 9-inch round cake pans.

2. **for the topping** Using your fingers, mix brown sugar, granulated sugar, flour, butter, and cinnamon in medium bowl until mixture resembles wet sand. Stir in pecans.

3. **for the cake** Whisk flour, baking powder, baking soda, cinnamon, and salt together in large bowl. In medium bowl, whisk sour cream, brown sugar, granulated sugar, eggs, and melted butter until smooth. Gently fold sour cream mixture into flour mixture until smooth (do not overmix; some streaks of flour might remain).

4. Scrape batter into prepared pans and smooth tops. Sprinkle topping evenly over both cakes.

5. Bake until topping looks crisp and toasted, and toothpick inserted into centers comes out with few crumbs attached, 25 to 30 minutes, rotating pans halfway through baking. Let cakes cool on wire rack for 15 minutes before serving.

## variations

quick lemon-blueberry coffee cake

Add 1 teaspoon grated lemon zest to flour mixture. Toss 2 cups fresh or frozen berries (do not thaw if frozen) with 1 tablespoon flour, then gently fold into batter.

quick apricot-orange coffee cake

Add 1 teaspoon grated orange zest to flour mixture, and gently fold 1 cup chopped dried apricots into batter.

cream cheese glaze
*makes about ¾ cup*

1½ cups (6 ounces) confectioners' sugar

3 tablespoons cream cheese, softened

3 tablespoons milk

1 teaspoon lemon juice

Pinch salt

Whisk all ingredients in bowl until smooth, then let sit until thickened, about 25 minutes. Drizzle glaze over top of completely cooled cake, letting it drip down sides. Let glaze set for 25 minutes before serving.

**to make ahead**
Following step 4, cover pans tightly with plastic wrap and refrigerate for up to 24 hours or freeze for up to 1 month. Bake cakes as directed, increasing baking time to 30 to 35 minutes if refrigerated, or 40 to 45 minutes if frozen (do not thaw before baking).

# sour cream coffee cake with brown sugar–pecan streusel

*why this recipe works* This ultrarich coffee cake is pure decadence, from its nutty topping and dramatic swirls of cinnamon sugar to its supremely moist, dense crumb. We cut softened butter into the dry ingredients for a tight, velvety crumb, and sour cream delivered distinct tang. Sprinkling a simple streusel over the batter in two layers created a dramatic swirling effect, and topping the cake off with more streusel (this time boosted with butter and pecans) gave it a crumbly crust. A fixed-bottom 10-inch tube pan (with a 10-cup capacity) is best for this recipe. Note that the streusel is divided into two parts—one for the inner swirls and one for the topping.

*makes 1 cake*
*total time: 1 hour 15 minutes*
*(plus 2 hours 30 minutes*
*cooling time)*

*streusel*
¾ cup (3¾ ounces) all-purpose flour

¾ cup (5¼ ounces) granulated sugar

½ cup packed (3½ ounces) dark brown sugar

2 tablespoons ground cinnamon

1 cup pecans, chopped

2 tablespoons unsalted butter, cut into 2 pieces and chilled

*cake*
1½ cups sour cream

4 large eggs

1 tablespoon vanilla extract

2¼ cups (11¼ ounces) all-purpose flour

1¼ cups (8¾ ounces) granulated sugar

1 tablespoon baking powder

¾ teaspoon baking soda

¾ teaspoon salt

12 tablespoons unsalted butter, cut into ½-inch cubes and softened but still cool

**1. for the streusel** Process flour, granulated sugar, ¼ cup brown sugar, and cinnamon in food processor until combined, about 15 seconds. Transfer 1¼ cups flour-sugar mixture to small bowl and stir in remaining ¼ cup brown sugar; set aside filling. Add pecans and butter to food processor and pulse until mixture resembles coarse meal, about 10 pulses. Set aside streusel.

**2. for the cake** Adjust oven rack to lowest position and heat oven to 350 degrees. Grease and flour 10-inch tube pan. Whisk 1 cup sour cream, eggs, and vanilla together in medium bowl.

**3.** Using stand mixer fitted with paddle, mix flour, sugar, baking powder, baking soda, and salt on low speed until combined, about 30 seconds. Add butter and remaining ½ cup sour cream and mix until dry ingredients are moistened and mixture resembles wet sand with few large butter pieces remaining, about 1½ minutes. Increase speed to medium and beat until batter comes together, about 10 seconds, scraping down sides of bowl with rubber spatula. Reduce speed to medium-low and gradually add egg mixture in 3 additions, beating for 20 seconds and scraping down sides after

each addition. Increase speed to medium-high and beat until batter is light and fluffy, about 1 minute.

**4.** Using rubber spatula, spread 2 cups batter in bottom of prepared pan and smooth surface. Sprinkle evenly with ¾ cup streusel filling (without butter or nuts). Repeat with another 2 cups batter and remaining ¾ cup streusel filling (without butter or nuts). Spread remaining batter over filling, then sprinkle with streusel topping (with butter and nuts).

**5.** Bake until cake feels firm to touch and skewer inserted in center comes out clean (bits of sugar from streusel may cling to skewer), 50 minutes to 1 hour, rotating cake halfway through baking. Let cake cool in pan on wire rack for 30 minutes. Gently invert cake onto rimmed baking sheet (cake will be streusel side down); remove tube pan, place wire rack on top of cake, and invert cake streusel side up. Let cool completely, about 2 hours, before serving.

**to make ahead**
Cake can be wrapped in aluminum foil and stored at room temperature for up to 5 days.

# olive oil cake

*why this recipe works* Don't let this cake's simple appearance fool you: Its fruity, slightly peppery olive oil flavor and beautifully plush, fine texture make it a treat worth enjoying at any time of day, particularly with brunch. In order to make sure our batter could support the most olive oil possible, we thoroughly whipped the eggs with sugar before incorporating the oil and dry ingredients, creating a stable but well-aerated batter. Supplementing the fresh, bright taste of olive oil with a bit of lemon zest created an especially bright flavor profile. We baked the cake in a springform pan, sprinkling it generously with sugar for a crackly-sweet crust. For the best flavor, use a fresh, high-quality extra-virgin olive oil. Our favorite supermarket option is California Olive Ranch Everyday Extra Virgin Olive Oil. If your springform pan is prone to leaking, place a rimmed baking sheet on the oven floor to catch any drips.

*makes 1 cake*
*total time: 1 hour*
*(plus 1 hour 45 minutes cooling time)*

1¾ cups (8¾ ounces) all-purpose flour

1 teaspoon baking powder

¾ teaspoon salt

3 large eggs

1¼ cups (8¾ ounces) plus 2 tablespoons sugar

¼ teaspoon grated lemon zest

¾ cup extra-virgin olive oil

¾ cup milk

1. Adjust oven rack to middle position and heat oven to 350 degrees. Grease 9-inch springform pan. Whisk flour, baking powder, and salt together in bowl.

2. Using stand mixer fitted with whisk attachment, whip eggs on medium speed until foamy, about 1 minute. Add 1¼ cups sugar and lemon zest, increase speed to high, and whip until mixture is fluffy and pale yellow, about 3 minutes. Reduce speed to medium and, with mixer running, slowly pour in oil. Mix until oil is fully incorporated, about 1 minute. Add half of flour mixture and mix on low speed until incorporated, about 1 minute, scraping down bowl as needed. Add milk and mix until combined, about 30 seconds. Add remaining flour mixture and mix until just incorporated, about 1 minute, scraping down bowl as needed.

3. Transfer batter to prepared pan; sprinkle remaining 2 tablespoons sugar over entire surface. Bake until cake is deep golden brown and toothpick inserted in center comes out with few crumbs attached, 40 to 45 minutes, rotating cake halfway through baking. Transfer pan to wire rack and let cool for 15 minutes. Remove side of pan and let cake cool completely, about 1½ hours. Cut into wedges and serve.

**to make ahead**
Cake can be wrapped in plastic wrap and stored at room temperature for up to 3 days.

# cider-glazed apple bundt cake

*why this recipe works* Delivering bright apple flavor and a temptingly moist crumb, this simple yet stunning Bundt cake demands a prominent place in your brunch spread. We maximized this cake's apple taste by shredding 1½ pounds of tart Granny Smiths and bolstering their flavor with an intense reduction of apple cider mixed into the batter, brushed onto the warm exterior of the baked cake, and stirred into an icing. Using a moderate amount of spices allowed the apple flavor to shine. Baking this fruity cake in a Bundt pan made all the difference, as the hole through the middle meant the dense batter baked through evenly and completely for a perfectly cooked cake. For the sake of efficiency, begin boiling the cider before assembling the rest of the ingredients. Reducing the cider to exactly 1 cup is important; if you accidentally overreduce it, make up the difference with water. To ensure that the icing has the proper consistency, we recommend weighing the confectioners' sugar. We like the tartness of Granny Smith apples in this recipe, but any variety of apple will work. You can shred the apples with the shredding disk of a food processor or on the large holes of a paddle or box grater.

*makes 1 cake*
*total time: 1 hour 45 minutes*
*(plus 2 hours 30 minutes cooling time)*

4 cups apple cider

3¾ cups (18¾ ounces) all-purpose flour

1½ teaspoons salt

1½ teaspoons baking powder

½ teaspoon baking soda

¾ teaspoon ground cinnamon

¼ teaspoon ground allspice

¾ cup (3 ounces) confectioners' sugar

16 tablespoons (2 sticks) unsalted butter, melted

1½ cups packed (10½ ounces) dark brown sugar

3 large eggs

2 teaspoons vanilla extract

1½ pounds Granny Smith apples, peeled, cored, and shredded (3 cups)

1. Bring cider to boil in 12-inch skillet over high heat; cook until reduced to 1 cup, 20 to 25 minutes. While cider is reducing, adjust oven rack to middle position and heat oven to 350 degrees. Grease and flour 12-cup nonstick Bundt pan. Whisk flour, salt, baking powder, baking soda, cinnamon, and allspice in large bowl until combined. Place confectioners' sugar in small bowl.

2. Add 2 tablespoons cider reduction to confectioners' sugar and whisk to form smooth icing. Cover with plastic wrap and set aside. Set aside 6 tablespoons cider reduction.

3. Pour remaining ½ cup cider reduction into large bowl; add melted butter, brown sugar, eggs, and vanilla and whisk until smooth. Pour cider mixture over flour mixture and stir with rubber spatula until almost fully combined (some streaks of flour will remain). Stir in apples and any accumulated juice until evenly distributed. Transfer mixture to prepared pan and smooth top. Bake until skewer inserted in center of cake comes out clean, 55 minutes to 1 hour 5 minutes, rotating cake halfway through baking.

4. Transfer pan to wire rack set in rimmed baking sheet. Brush exposed surface of cake lightly with 1 tablespoon reserved cider reduction. Let cake cool for 10 minutes. Invert cake onto wire rack and remove pan. Brush top and sides of cake with remaining 5 tablespoons reserved cider reduction. Let cake cool for 20 minutes. Stir icing to loosen, then drizzle evenly over cake. Let cake cool completely, at least 2 hours, before serving.

**to make ahead**
Cooled cake can be wrapped loosely in plastic wrap and stored at room temperature for up to 3 days.

brunch
sides

# nectarine, grape, and blueberry fruit salad with orange and cardamom

*why this recipe works* Fruit salad shouldn't be complicated, and thanks to a few carefully chosen ingredients, this recipe and its variations capitalize on fruit's natural sweetness for a refreshing side to any brunch. Choosing a colorful blend of fruits offered an enticing range of flavors and textures, and by macerating them in a moderate amount of sugar muddled with a few complementary flavorings like herbs, spices, and citrus juice, we created nuanced, unified salads in no time. Riper fruits require more acid to balance their sweetness, so add the lime juice to taste. Start with 1 tablespoon, then add 1 teaspoon at a time as necessary.

*serves 4 to 6*
*total time: 30 minutes*

4 teaspoons sugar

1 teaspoon grated orange zest

⅛ teaspoon ground cardamom

1½ pounds nectarines, halved, pitted, and cut into ½-inch pieces

9 ounces large green grapes, halved (about 1½ cups)

10 ounces (2 cups) blueberries

1–2 tablespoons lime juice

Combine sugar, orange zest, and cardamom in large bowl. Using rubber spatula, press mixture into side of bowl until sugar becomes damp, about 30 seconds. Gently toss fruit with sugar mixture until combined. Let stand at room temperature, stirring occasionally, until fruit releases its juices, 15 to 30 minutes. Stir in lime juice to taste, and serve.

## variations

cantaloupe, plum, and cherry fruit salad with mint and vanilla

4 teaspoons sugar

1–2 tablespoons minced fresh mint

¼ teaspoon vanilla extract

3 cups cantaloupe, cut into ½-inch pieces

2 plums, halved, pitted, and cut into ½-inch pieces

8 ounces fresh sweet cherries, pitted and halved

1–2 tablespoons lime juice

Combine sugar and mint to taste in large bowl. Using rubber spatula, press mixture into side of bowl until sugar becomes damp, about 30 seconds; add vanilla. Gently toss fruit with sugar mixture until combined. Let sit at room temperature, stirring occasionally, until fruit releases its juices, 15 to 30 minutes. Stir in lime juice to taste, and serve.

honeydew, mango, and raspberry fruit salad with lime and ginger

4 teaspoons sugar

2 teaspoons grated lime zest plus 1–2 tablespoons juice

Pinch cayenne pepper (optional)

3 cups honeydew melon, cut into ½-inch pieces

1 mango, peeled, pitted, and cut into ½-inch pieces

1–2 teaspoons grated fresh ginger

5 ounces (1 cup) raspberries

Combine sugar, lime zest, and cayenne, if using, in large bowl. Using rubber spatula, press mixture into side of bowl until sugar becomes damp, about 30 seconds. Gently toss honeydew, mango, and ginger to taste with sugar mixture until combined. Let sit at room temperature, stirring occasionally, until fruit releases its juices, 15 to 30 minutes. Gently stir in raspberries. Stir in lime juice to taste, and serve.

peach, blackberry, and strawberry fruit salad with basil and pepper

4 teaspoons sugar

2 tablespoons chopped fresh basil

½ teaspoon pepper

1½ pounds peaches, halved, pitted, and cut into ½-inch pieces

10 ounces (2 cups) blackberries

10 ounces strawberries, hulled and quartered lengthwise (2 cups)

1–2 tablespoons lime juice

Combine sugar, basil, and pepper in large bowl. Using rubber spatula, press mixture into side of bowl until sugar becomes damp, about 30 seconds. Gently toss fruit with sugar mixture until combined. Let sit at room temperature, stirring occasionally, until fruit releases its juices, 15 to 30 minutes. Stir in lime juice to taste, and serve.

# almond-raisin granola

*why this recipe works* We love rounding out a rich brunch with a cool bowl of yogurt topped off with this satisfyingly chunky, deeply flavored granola. Unlike the underwhelming (and overpriced) grocery store options, this easy, make ahead–friendly granola brings home big, satisfying oat clusters and a perfectly crisp texture. The secret to keeping the sweet, toasty clusters in appealingly large chunks was spreading and firmly packing the granola into a rimmed baking sheet and cooking it undisturbed. A mixture of maple syrup, brown sugar, vanilla, and salt promised a darkly sweet, nutty flavor that mirrored the toasty taste of the hearty rolled oats and chopped almonds. We baked the oat-nut mixture in a moderate oven and were rewarded with fragrant granola "bark" that we could break into crunchy hunks of any size. To finish, we stirred raisins into the cooled granola for bursts of juicy sweetness. With a recipe this simple, coming up with a few more tempting flavor options was a breeze. Do not use quick oats here. Chopping the almonds by hand is best for superior crunch, but you can substitute an equal amount of slivered or sliced almonds, if desired. Use a single type of your favorite dried fruit or a combination.

*makes about 9 cups*
*total time: 45 minutes*
*(plus 1 hour cooling time)*

½ cup vegetable oil

⅓ cup maple syrup

⅓ cup packed (2⅓ ounces) light brown sugar

4 teaspoons vanilla extract

½ teaspoon salt

5 cups (15 ounces) old-fashioned rolled oats

2 cups (10 ounces) raw almonds, chopped coarse

2 cups (10 ounces) raisins, chopped

1. Adjust oven rack to upper-middle position and heat oven to 325 degrees. Line rimmed baking sheet with parchment paper. Spray parchment with vegetable oil spray.

2. Whisk oil, maple syrup, sugar, vanilla, and salt together in large bowl. Fold in oats and almonds until thoroughly combined.

3. Transfer oat mixture to prepared sheet and spread across entire surface of sheet in even layer. Using stiff metal spatula, press down firmly on oat mixture until very compact. Bake until lightly browned, 35 to 40 minutes, rotating sheet halfway through baking.

4. Transfer sheet to wire rack and let granola cool completely, about 1 hour. Break cooled granola into pieces of desired size. Stir in raisins and serve.

**variations**

apricot-orange granola
Substitute 1 cup raw pepitas, chopped coarse, for almonds and dried apricots for raisins. Add 1 tablespoon grated orange zest to oil mixture in step 2.

cherry–chocolate chip granola
Substitute dried cherries for raisins. Add 1 cup mini semisweet chocolate chips to mixture with dried cherries in step 4.

honey-pecan granola
Substitute honey for sugar and pecans for almonds. Add 1 tablespoon ground cinnamon to oil mixture in step 2.

salted caramel–peanut granola
Omit raisins. Increase salt to 1½ teaspoons. Substitute ¾ cup jarred caramel sauce for sugar and unsalted dry-roasted peanuts for almonds.

**to make ahead**
Granola can be stored at room temperature for up to 2 weeks.

# baked cheese grits

*why this recipe works*  Corn grits can be prepared in a variety of ways, but this lush baked version brings out the best in grits' sweet corn flavor. We opted for old-fashioned grits because, unlike their quick counterparts, they turn creamy but still retain some appealing coarseness through cooking. Simmering the grits in cream and salted water gave them full, deep flavor while some softened chopped onion and a hit of hot sauce rounded out the edges. Eggs added richness and structure, promising a texture somewhere between polenta and custardy spoonbread, and a cup of shredded extra-sharp cheddar delivered welcome tang. Spread into a baking dish, topped off with more cheese, and baked, these simple grits emerged just the creamy, rich accompaniment we craved with all our favorite brunch dishes. Do not substitute quick grits, which are finely ground and presteamed, for the old-fashioned grits called for here. Quick grits do not offer enough texture or body and will make for a gluey casserole. You can substitute other cheeses, such as smoked cheddar or smoked gouda, for the extra-sharp cheddar, if desired.

*serves 6 to 8*
*total time: 1 hour 15 minutes*

3 tablespoons unsalted butter

1 onion, chopped fine

4½ cups water

1½ cups heavy cream

1 teaspoon salt

¾ teaspoon hot sauce

1½ cups old-fashioned grits

8 ounces extra-sharp cheddar cheese, shredded (2 cups)

4 large eggs, lightly beaten

¼ teaspoon pepper

1. Adjust oven rack to middle position and heat oven to 350 degrees. Grease 13 by 9-inch baking dish with 1 tablespoon butter.

2. Melt remaining 2 tablespoons butter in Dutch oven over medium heat. Add onion and cook, stirring often, until softened, 5 to 7 minutes. Add water, cream, salt, and hot sauce. Cover pot and bring mixture to boil.

3. Remove lid and slowly whisk in grits. Reduce heat to low and cook uncovered, stirring often, until grits are thick and creamy, about 15 minutes. Off heat, whisk in 1 cup cheddar, eggs, and pepper.

4. Pour mixture into prepared dish and smooth top with rubber spatula. Sprinkle remaining 1 cup cheddar over top. Bake until top is browned and grits are hot, 35 to 45 minutes. Remove grits from oven and let cool for 10 minutes before serving.

### variation

baked cheese grits with red bell pepper and pepper jack
Add 1 stemmed, seeded, and finely chopped red bell pepper to pot with onion in step 2 and increase cooking time to 8 to 10 minutes. Substitute pepper Jack for cheddar.

# home fries

*why this recipe works* Home fries may be a common brunch side, but this recipe—with its impossibly crisp spuds, perfectly cooked onions, and enough food to satisfy a small crowd—is uncommonly good. Rather than prepare batch after batch of skillet-fried potatoes, we moved our cooking to a rimmed baking sheet, allowing us to prepare over 3 pounds of potatoes in one go. Briefly parboiling cut-up russet potatoes with a touch of baking soda helped rough up their exteriors, turning them starchy for speedy browning while keeping the interiors nearly raw. Tossing the drained potatoes with kosher salt over low heat further released that exterior starch so when the spuds hit the baking sheet—preheated in a superhot oven to mimic the sear of a skillet—they quickly developed a distinct browned crust. Tossing the potatoes with a touch of cayenne contributed some appealing heat and butter promoted deeper browning and rich flavor. Roasted in the oven, the potatoes turned golden brown and developed light, fluffy interiors. Because all good home fries are served with sweet bites of onion stirred in, we added diced onions to the center of the pan in the last 20 minutes of oven time and allowed them to soften and steam, buffered by the potatoes to prevent burning. We finished off the home fries with minced chives to reinforce and freshen the onions' flavor. Don't skip the baking soda here—it's critical for home fries with just the right crispy texture.

*serves 6 to 8*
*total time: 1 hour*

3½ pounds russet potatoes, peeled and cut into ¾-inch pieces

½ teaspoon baking soda

3 tablespoons unsalted butter, cut into 12 pieces

Kosher salt and pepper

Pinch cayenne pepper

3 tablespoons vegetable oil

2 onions, cut into ½-inch pieces

3 tablespoons minced chives

1. Adjust oven rack to lowest position, place rimmed baking sheet on rack, and heat oven to 500 degrees.

2. Bring 2½ quarts water to boil in Dutch oven over high heat. Add potatoes and baking soda. Return to boil and cook for 1 minute. Drain potatoes. Return potatoes to pot and place over low heat. Cook, shaking pot occasionally, until any surface moisture has evaporated, about 2 minutes. Off heat, add butter, 1½ teaspoons salt, and cayenne; using rubber spatula, mix until potatoes are coated with thick, starchy paste, about 30 seconds.

3. Remove sheet from oven and drizzle with 2 tablespoons oil. Transfer potatoes to sheet and spread into even layer. Roast for 15 minutes. While potatoes roast, combine onions, ½ teaspoon salt, and remaining 1 tablespoon oil in bowl.

4. Remove sheet from oven. Using thin, sharp metal spatula, scrape and turn potatoes. Clear about 8 by 5-inch space in center of sheet and add onion mixture. Roast for 15 minutes.

5. Scrape and turn again, mixing onions into potatoes. Continue to roast until potatoes are well browned and onions are softened and beginning to brown, 5 to 10 minutes. Stir in chives and season with salt and pepper to taste. Serve immediately.

# classic hash browns

*why this recipe works*  Homemade hash browns can be a real chore, with the shredded potato cake often falling apart when you try to flip it and the exterior burning before the interior is fully cooked. Our version takes the fuss out of this greasy-spoon favorite, delivering gorgeously golden hash browns with a crisp yet creamy texture every time. Grated russet potatoes beat out other spuds and slicing methods: These potatoes adhered well, browned beautifully, and had the most pronounced potato flavor. Grating them raw and squeezing out their moisture produced hash browns that held together while cooking, had a tender interior, and boasted an attractive, deeply browned crust. We ensured deep, distinct browning by pressing the grated potatoes into the bottom of a sizzling hot buttered skillet and then we successfully flipped the cake in one piece with the help of a plate. To finish, we folded the family-size cake in half, gave it one last minute in the pan, then served it in generous wedges. We prefer hash browns prepared with potatoes that have been cut with the large shredding disk of a food processor, but a box grater can also be used. To prevent the potatoes from turning brown, grate them just before cooking. Garnish with chopped scallions or chives before serving, if desired.

*serves 4*
*total time: 30 minutes*

1 pound russet potatoes, peeled and shredded

Salt and pepper

2 tablespoons unsalted butter

1. Wrap shredded potatoes in clean dish towel and squeeze thoroughly to remove excess moisture. Toss potatoes with ¼ teaspoon salt and season with pepper to taste.

2. Melt 1 tablespoon butter in 10-inch skillet over medium-high heat until it begins to brown, swirling to coat skillet. Scatter potatoes evenly over entire skillet and press to flatten. Reduce heat to medium and cook until dark golden brown and crisp, 7 to 8 minutes.

3. Slide hash browns onto large plate. Melt remaining 1 tablespoon butter in now-empty skillet, swirling to coat pan. Invert hash browns onto second plate and slide, browned side up, back into skillet. Continue to cook over medium heat until bottom is dark golden brown and crisp, 5 to 6 minutes longer.

4. Fold hash brown cake in half; cook for 1 minute. Slide onto plate or cutting board, cut into wedges, and serve immediately.

# roasted asparagus

*why this recipe works* Roasted asparagus brings some color and fresh flavor to any brunch table, and this recipe's roasting technique ensures a side of perfectly cooked spears that are crisp yet tender, verdant yet perfectly browned. By selecting ½-inch-thick asparagus spears, trimming off their tough ends, and peeling away the woody skin to expose the creamy interior, we quickly set ourselves up for roasting success. To keep this simple recipe hands-off, we kept it all in the oven, first imparting a hard sear on our spears by preheating the baking sheet, then by resisting the urge to give it a shake during roasting. The result? Intense, flavorful browning on one side of the asparagus and vibrant green on the other. For some complementary seasoning, we took our cue from Italian cuisine, preparing a bright garnish of minced fresh herbs called a gremolata. Fresh mint, fresh parsley, orange zest, minced garlic, and a hit of cayenne constituted our first version, and the more classic combination of tarragon, parsley, lemon zest, and garlic our second. Both reinforced the stalks' flavor and gave our simple brunch side a more distinct presence. This recipe works best with thick asparagus spears that are between ½ and ¾ inch in diameter. Do not use pencil-thin asparagus; it overcooks too easily.

*serves 4 to 6*
*total time: 30 minutes*

**2 pounds thick asparagus, trimmed**

**2 tablespoons plus 2 teaspoons extra-virgin olive oil**

**½ teaspoon salt**

**¼ teaspoon pepper**

1. Adjust oven rack to lowest position, place rimmed baking sheet on rack, and heat oven to 500 degrees. Peel bottom halves of asparagus spears until white flesh is exposed, then toss with 2 tablespoons oil, salt, and pepper.

2. Transfer asparagus to preheated sheet and spread into single layer. Roast, without moving asparagus, until undersides of spears are browned, tops are bright green, and tip of paring knife inserted at base of largest spear meets little resistance, 8 to 10 minutes. Transfer asparagus to serving platter and drizzle with remaining 2 teaspoons oil. Serve.

## variations

### roasted asparagus with mint-orange gremolata

Combine 2 tablespoons minced fresh mint, 2 tablespoons minced fresh parsley, 2 teaspoons grated orange zest, 1 minced garlic clove, and pinch cayenne pepper in bowl. Sprinkle gremolata over asparagus before serving.

### roasted asparagus with tarragon-lemon gremolata

Combine 2 tablespoons minced fresh tarragon, 2 tablespoons minced fresh parsley, 2 teaspoons grated lemon zest, and 1 minced garlic clove in bowl. Sprinkle gremolata over asparagus before serving.

# roasted green beans with pecorino and pine nuts

*why this recipe works* Roasting is a simple way to transform fresh green beans, which can be a little tough, into a sweet, crisp, verdant side, and this recipe achieves that while keeping your stovetop open for preparing the rest of your brunch menu. To season the slender beans and keep them perfectly moist, we tossed them with oil, sugar, salt, and pepper before sealing them under foil to gently steam in the oven. Removing the foil with 10 minutes to go caramelized the sugar for some subtle, tasty browning. To add some zip to the nicely blistered beans, we tossed them with a lemony vinaigrette, microwaving garlic and lemon zest with oil to bloom their flavors and tame the garlic's raw bite. We topped the beans with salty, sharp Pecorino and crunchy toasted pine nuts for a savory, nutty finish. Use the large holes of a box grater to shred the Pecorino.

*serves 4 to 6*
*total time: 30 minutes*

1½ pounds green beans, trimmed

5½ tablespoons extra-virgin olive oil

¾ teaspoon sugar

Kosher salt and pepper

2 garlic cloves, minced

1 teaspoon grated lemon zest plus 4 teaspoons juice

1 teaspoon Dijon mustard

2 tablespoons chopped fresh basil

1½ ounces Pecorino Romano cheese, shredded (½ cup)

¼ cup pine nuts, toasted

1. Adjust oven rack to lowest position and heat oven to 475 degrees. Toss green beans with 1½ tablespoons oil, sugar, ¾ teaspoon salt, and ½ teaspoon pepper. Transfer to rimmed baking sheet and spread into single layer.

2. Cover sheet tightly with aluminum foil and roast for 10 minutes. Remove foil and continue to roast until green beans are spotty brown, about 10 minutes, stirring halfway through roasting.

3. Meanwhile, combine garlic, lemon zest, and remaining ¼ cup oil in medium bowl and microwave until bubbling, about 1 minute. Let mixture steep for 1 minute, then whisk in lemon juice, mustard, ¼ teaspoon salt, and ¼ teaspoon pepper until combined.

4. Transfer green beans to bowl with dressing, add basil, and toss to combine. Season with salt and pepper to taste. Transfer green beans to serving platter and sprinkle with Pecorino and pine nuts. Serve.

## variation

### roasted green beans with almonds and mint

Omit Pecorino. Substitute 1 teaspoon lime zest and 4 teaspoons lime juice for lemon zest and juice, ¼ cup torn fresh mint leaves for basil, and ¼ cup whole blanched almonds, toasted and chopped, for pine nuts.

# corn fritters

*why this recipe works* These Southern-style corn fritters boast unapologetic fresh corn flavor and an irresistible crisp exterior, making them the perfect sweet accompaniment to a sprawling savory brunch. To keep the fritters corn-focused, we pulsed two ears' worth of kernels into a puree, which we used to thicken the batter. A moderate amount of flour and a touch of cornstarch kept the texture light while also ensuring that the fritters fried up crisp and lacy. After browning more kernels in a skillet, we stirred in the puree to drive off excess moisture and deepen its sweet flavor. Chives, Parmesan, and cayenne offered a deep, savory counterpoint. A hot skillet with just enough oil to cover its cooking surface produced bite-size fritters that were beautifully golden brown (and not greasy) in every last nook and cranny. Serve with sour cream or our Maple-Chipotle Mayonnaise or Red Pepper Mayonnaise (recipes follow), if desired.

*makes 12 fritters*
*total time: 30 minutes*

4 ears corn, kernels cut from cobs (3 cups)

1 teaspoon plus ½ cup vegetable oil

Salt and pepper

¼ cup all-purpose flour

¼ cup finely minced chives

2 tablespoons grated Parmesan cheese

1 tablespoon cornstarch

Pinch cayenne pepper

1 large egg, lightly beaten

**1.** Process 1½ cups corn kernels in food processor to uniformly coarse puree, 15 to 20 seconds, scraping down sides of bowl halfway through processing. Set aside.

**2.** Heat 1 teaspoon oil in 12-inch nonstick skillet over medium-high heat until shimmering. Add remaining 1½ cups corn kernels and ⅛ teaspoon salt and cook, stirring frequently, until light golden, 3 to 4 minutes. Transfer to medium bowl.

**3.** Return skillet to medium heat, add corn puree, and cook, stirring frequently with heatproof spatula, until puree is consistency of thick oatmeal (puree clings to spatula rather than dripping off), about 5 minutes. Transfer puree to bowl with kernels and stir to combine. Rinse skillet and dry with paper towels.

**4.** Stir flour, 3 tablespoons chives, Parmesan, cornstarch, cayenne, ¼ teaspoon salt, and ⅛ teaspoon pepper into corn mixture until well combined. Gently stir in egg until incorporated.

**5.** Line rimmed baking sheet with paper towels. Heat remaining ½ cup oil in now-empty skillet over medium heat until shimmering. Drop six 2-tablespoon portions of batter into skillet. Press with spatula to flatten into 2½- to 3-inch disks. Fry until deep golden brown on both sides, 2 to 3 minutes per side. Transfer fritters to prepared sheet. Repeat with remaining batter.

**6.** Transfer fritters to large plate or platter, sprinkle with remaining 1 tablespoon chives, and serve immediately.

## maple-chipotle mayonnaise
*makes ⅔ cup*

½ cup mayonnaise

1 tablespoon maple syrup

1 tablespoon minced canned chipotle chile in adobo sauce

½ teaspoon Dijon mustard

Combine all ingredients in bowl.

## red pepper mayonnaise
*makes about 1¼ cups*

1½ teaspoons lemon juice

1 garlic clove, minced

¾ cup jarred roasted red peppers, rinsed and patted dry

½ cup mayonnaise

2 teaspoons tomato paste

Salt

Combine lemon juice and garlic in small bowl and let stand for 15 minutes. Process red peppers, mayonnaise, tomato paste, and lemon juice mixture in food processor until smooth, about 15 seconds, scraping down sides of bowl as needed. Season with salt to taste. Refrigerate until thickened, about 2 hours.

# oven-fried bacon

*why this recipe works* This bacon-making method is a brunch game changer. A couple strips of bacon are always a welcome accompaniment to a slice of quiche or a stack of pancakes, but this essential side requires frequent monitoring when cooked on the stovetop, and the hot grease can be messy and dangerous. By moving the whole production to the oven, we were able to prepare reliably crisp, hands-off bacon en masse—no splattering fat and no lingering odor in the kitchen. We spread a dozen strips over a broad rimmed baking sheet, the sides proving just high enough to contain the rendered fat while promoting even exposure to the heat. The steady blast from the oven cooked the bacon evenly, so rather than flipping all of the strips we simply needed to rotate the pan once halfway through cooking. A large rimmed baking sheet is important here to contain the rendered bacon fat. This recipe is easy to double for a crowd: Simply double the amount of bacon and use two rimmed baking sheets. However, if you're cooking more than one sheet of bacon at a time, be sure to rotate the sheets and switch their oven positions once about halfway through cooking. You can use thin- or thick-cut bacon here, though the cooking times will vary.

*serves 4 to 6*
*total time: 30 minutes*

**12 slices bacon**

Adjust oven rack to middle position and heat oven to 400 degrees. Arrange bacon on rimmed baking sheet. Cook until fat begins to render, 5 to 6 minutes; rotate sheet. Continue cooking until bacon is crisp and brown, 5 to 6 minutes for thin-cut bacon or 8 to 10 minutes for thick-cut bacon. Transfer bacon to paper towel–lined plate, drain, and serve.

**variation**

maple-glazed oven-fried bacon
After roasting, pour off most of grease and drizzle maple syrup over each strip (¼ cup total). Return sheet to oven and continue cooking for 2 to 3 minutes, or until maple syrup begins to bubble. Transfer with tongs to paper towel–lined plate, drain, and serve.

# homemade breakfast sausage

*why this recipe works* There's no comparing commercially made breakfast sausage with these homemade patties: Our recipe produces meaty, deeply seasoned sausage that can easily be made ahead of time, which makes these juicy, browned patties an effortless addition to any brunch menu. To make these standout sausages at home, we started with convenient ground pork with some fat in it (lean meat proved neither fatty nor flavorful enough) and amped up its mild flavor with classic breakfast sausage seasonings: garlic, sage, thyme, and cayenne pepper. A spoonful of maple syrup sweetened the patties with its complexity and warmth. To form the patties, we simply kneaded the pork and seasonings together until they were just incorporated, thereby keeping the finished texture moist and tender. Once they were formed, we had the option of searing them to savory, fragrant perfection in minutes or storing the patties in the fridge or freezer for later use. Avoid lean or extra-lean ground pork; it makes the sausage dry, crumbly, and less flavorful.

*makes 16 patties*
*total time: 30 minutes*

2 pounds ground pork

1 tablespoon maple syrup

2 teaspoons dried sage

1½ teaspoons pepper

1 teaspoon salt

1 garlic clove, minced

½ teaspoon dried thyme

⅛ teaspoon cayenne pepper

2 tablespoons unsalted butter

**1.** Combine pork, maple syrup, sage, pepper, salt, garlic, thyme, and cayenne in large bowl. Gently mix with your hands until well combined. Using greased ¼-cup measure, divide mixture into 16 patties and place on rimmed baking sheet. Cover patties with plastic wrap, then gently flatten each one to ½-inch thickness.

**2.** Melt 1 tablespoon butter in 12-inch nonstick skillet over medium heat. Cook half of patties until well browned and cooked through, 3 to 5 minutes per side. Transfer to paper towel–lined plate and tent with aluminum foil. Wipe out skillet. Repeat with remaining butter and patties. Serve.

**to make ahead**
Raw sausage patties can be refrigerated, covered, for up to 24 hours or frozen for up to 1 month. To cook frozen patties, proceed with step 2, cooking patties for 7 to 9 minutes per side.

# tricolor salad with balsamic vinaigrette

*why this recipe works* A special brunch demands a simple but thoughtful salad, not just a smattering of greenery. This effortless, versatile side is robust, crisp, and peppery—an easy addition to round out any menu. Most takes on this Italian classic feature a pared-down vinaigrette of just extra-virgin olive oil, red wine vinegar, and salt, but we liked the sweet, complex addition of balsamic vinegar as well. Arugula, radicchio, and Belgian endive are the classic trio in this salad—their colors are meant to reflect the bands in the Italian flag—and the understated dressing allows each ingredient's personality to shine. Cutting the pleasantly bitter radicchio into 1-inch pieces and the mild, crunchy endive heads into 2-inch pieces ensured that every forkful delivered the right balance of flavors and textures. With our dressing and greens at the ready, a quick toss was all the work needed to assemble this bold salad. Toss the dressing with the greens just before serving. Our favorite supermarket balsamic vinegar is Bertolli Balsamic Vinegar of Modena.

*serves 8*
*total time: 15 minutes*

**7 teaspoons balsamic vinegar**

**2 teaspoons red wine vinegar**

**Salt and pepper**

**6 tablespoons extra-virgin olive oil**

**5 ounces baby arugula (5 cups)**

**1 head radicchio (10 ounces), cut into 1-inch pieces**

**2 heads Belgian endive (8 ounces), cut into 2-inch pieces**

Whisk balsamic vinegar, red wine vinegar, ¼ teaspoon salt, and ⅛ teaspoon pepper in small bowl. Whisking constantly, drizzle in oil. In large bowl, toss arugula with radicchio and endive. Just before serving, whisk dressing to re-emulsify, then drizzle over salad and toss gently to coat.

# citrus salad with bitter greens

*why this recipe works* This light and refreshing salad sets pieces of fresh orange and grapefruit against a backdrop of spicy watercress and crisp endive, a combination that makes it a seamless addition to brunches sweet and savory alike. To keep the salad crisp and lively, we drained the sliced fruit, but rather than let those bright juices go to waste, we put them to use in a zippy vinaigrette we sweetened with honey. A generous handful of parsley added a fresh, herbal dimension to the salad, and shaved Parmesan offered a nutty, salty finish.

*serves 8*
*total time: 30 minutes*

2 grapefruits

2 large oranges

¼ cup red wine vinegar

1 shallot, minced

1 tablespoon honey

¼ teaspoon salt

⅛ teaspoon pepper

⅔ cup extra-virgin olive oil

12 ounces watercress, trimmed (12 cups)

3 heads Belgian endive (4 ounces each), leaves separated and cut into 2-inch pieces

¼ cup fresh parsley leaves

2 ounces Parmesan cheese, shaved

**1.** Cut away peel and pith from grapefruits and oranges. Quarter grapefruits and oranges, then slice crosswise into ¼-inch-thick pieces. Transfer fruit to colander, set over bowl to catch drained liquid and set aside until ready to serve.

**2.** Whisk 1 tablespoon drained citrus juice, vinegar, shallot, honey, salt, and pepper together in medium bowl. Whisking constantly, drizzle in olive oil.

**3.** In large bowl, gently combine watercress, endive, and parsley. Just before serving, add drained fruit, discarding remaining drained juice. Whisk dressing to re-emulsify, then drizzle over salad and toss gently to coat. Garnish individual portions with Parmesan.

# conversions and equivalents

Some say cooking is a science and an art. We would say that geography has a hand in it, too. Flours and sugars manufactured in the United Kingdom and elsewhere will feel and taste different from those manufactured in the United States. So we cannot promise that the pie crust you bake in Canada or England will taste the same as a pie crust baked in the States, but we can offer guidelines for converting weights and measures. We also recommend that you rely on your instincts when making our recipes. Refer to the visual cues provided. If the pie dough hasn't "come together," as described, you may need to add more water—even if the recipe doesn't tell you to. You be the judge.

The recipes in this book were developed using standard U.S. measures following U.S. government guidelines. The charts below offer equivalents for U.S. and metric measures. All conversions are approximate and have been rounded up or down to the nearest whole number. For example:

1 teaspoon  =  4.9292 milliliters, rounded up to 5 milliliters
1 ounce  =  28.3495 grams, rounded down to 28 grams

## volume conversions

| u.s. | metric |
| --- | --- |
| 1 teaspoon | 5 milliliters |
| 2 teaspoons | 10 milliliters |
| 1 tablespoon | 15 milliliters |
| 2 tablespoons | 30 milliliters |
| ¼ cup | 59 milliliters |
| ⅓ cup | 79 milliliters |
| ½ cup | 118 milliliters |
| ¾ cup | 177 milliliters |
| 1 cup | 237 milliliters |
| 1¼ cups | 296 milliliters |
| 1½ cups | 355 milliliters |
| 2 cups (1 pint) | 473 milliliters |
| 2½ cups | 591 milliliters |
| 3 cups | 710 milliliters |
| 4 cups (1 quart) | 0.946 liter |
| 1.06 quarts | 1 liter |
| 4 quarts (1 gallon) | 3.8 liters |

## weight conversions

| ounces | grams |
| --- | --- |
| ½ | 14 |
| ¾ | 21 |
| 1 | 28 |
| 1½ | 43 |
| 2 | 57 |
| 2½ | 71 |
| 3 | 85 |
| 3½ | 99 |
| 4 | 113 |
| 4½ | 128 |
| 5 | 142 |
| 6 | 170 |
| 7 | 198 |
| 8 | 227 |
| 9 | 255 |
| 10 | 283 |
| 12 | 340 |
| 16 (1 pound) | 454 |

## conversion for common baking ingredients

Baking is an exacting science. Because measuring by weight is far more accurate than measuring by volume, and thus more likely to produce reliable results, in our recipes we provide ounce measures in addition to cup measures for many ingredients. Refer to the chart below to convert these measures into grams.

| ingredient | ounces | grams |
|---|---|---|
| **flour** | | |
| 1 cup all-purpose flour* | 5 | 142 |
| 1 cup cake flour | 4 | 113 |
| 1 cup whole-wheat flour | 5½ | 156 |
| **sugar** | | |
| 1 cup granulated (white) sugar | 7 | 198 |
| 1 cup packed brown sugar (light or dark) | 7 | 198 |
| 1 cup confectioners' sugar | 4 | 113 |
| **cocoa powder** | | |
| 1 cup cocoa powder | 3 | 85 |
| **butter†** | | |
| 4 tablespoons (½ stick, or ¼ cup) | 2 | 57 |
| 8 tablespoons (1 stick, or ½ cup) | 4 | 113 |
| 16 tablespoons (2 sticks, or 1 cup) | 8 | 227 |

\* *U.S. all-purpose flour, the most frequently used flour in this book, does not contain leaveners, as some European flours do. These leavened flours are called self-rising or self-raising. If you are using self-rising flour, take this into consideration before adding leavening to a recipe.*

† *In the United States, butter is sold both salted and unsalted. We generally recommend unsalted butter. If you are using salted butter, take this into consideration before adding salt to a recipe.*

### oven temperatures

| fahrenheit | celsius | gas mark |
|---|---|---|
| 225 | 105 | ¼ |
| 250 | 120 | ½ |
| 275 | 135 | 1 |
| 300 | 150 | 2 |
| 325 | 165 | 3 |
| 350 | 180 | 4 |
| 375 | 190 | 5 |
| 400 | 200 | 6 |
| 425 | 220 | 7 |
| 450 | 230 | 8 |
| 475 | 245 | 9 |

### converting temperatures from an instant-read thermometer

We include doneness temperatures in many of the recipes in this book. We recommend an instant-read thermometer for the job. Refer to the table at left to convert Fahrenheit degrees to Celsius. Or, for temperatures not represented in the chart, use this simple formula:

Subtract 32 degrees from the Fahrenheit reading, then divide the result by 1.8 to find the Celsius reading. For example: "Roast chicken until thighs register 175 degrees."

To convert
175°F − 32 = 143°
143° ÷ 1.8 = 79.44°C, rounded down to 79°C

# index

Note: Page references in *italics* indicate photographs.